PATHWAY TO TRAUMA RECOVERY

TRANSFORM PAIN INTO POWER: OVERCOME THE MYSTERY

WELLNESS COACH LIZ BLANDING

COACH MICHAEL BART MATHEWS

The Mathews Entrepreneur Group Inc
We Create Books Division
www.tmeginc.com

THE
MATHEWS
ENTREPRENEUR
GROUP, INC.

PATHWAY TO TRAUMA RECOVERY

From the empowering coauthors, our words do reflect,

Our life-changing stories will be hard to reject,

We learned from our past and chose to keep going,

We are always growing; may our stories keep flowing,

Deep down in our hearts, this may be a heavy burden,

Our stories will help others; that is for certain,

We stepped out on faith to share with the world,

Reaching out to everyone, sharing wisdom and pearls,

The Universe has prepared us for this moment in time,

Because we are the vessel, leaving no one behind!

Coach Michael Bart Mathews

Table of Contents

ACKNOWLEDGEMENTS i

TESTIMONIAL/PRAISE ii

FOREWORD vi

INTRODUCTION 1

CHAPTER ONE
A FAMILY SECRET - THE IMPACT OF UNRESOLVED
TRAUMA
WELLNESS COACH LIZ BLANDING (USA) 4

CHAPTER TWO
HOW TO WIN IN THE GAME OF LIFE
MICHAEL BART MATHEWS (USA)....................................20

CHAPTER THREE
FACED DEFEAT BUT NEVER DEFEATED
KGABO LUCIA MANTHATA (SOUTH AFRICA).................36

CHAPTER FOUR
MY ADVERSITIES BECAME MY SEEDS OF GREATNESS
SHERRI PICKET (USA)..53

CHAPTER FIVE
NAVIGATING BULLYING PATHWAYS TO STRENGTH
AND HEALING
ANNE KRISTINE AKSNES (NETHERLANDS) 66

CHAPTER SIX
IF GOD WOULD NOT LET ME DIE
I HAD TO LEARN HOW TO LIVE
TRACY WHITT, CARC (USA)..80

CHAPTER SEVEN
FROM VULNERABLE TO VALUABLE
BELINDA OOSTHUIZEN (SOUTH AFRICA) 96

CHAPTER EIGHT
ROAD TO RECOVERY- THE RUNNING GIRL
LAMIS CHKEIR (LEBANON)..115

CHAPTER NINE
MY PUSH AND PRESS TO GREATNESS
BEVERLY LARUE (USA) 131

CHAPTER TEN
'BEAUTY FOR ASHES'
DELPHINE LYN HARRIS (USA)..145

CHAPTER ELEVEN
FROM A CATERPILLAR
TIMMY YOUNG (USA) 160

CHAPTER TWELVE
THE MIND WITH TOGETHERNESS, HISTORICALLY,
TAKES YOU WHERE YOUR TALENTS ALONE CAN'T
DR. JOESEPH WEBB III (USA) 175

CHAPTER THIRTEEN
DRIVEN BY PURPOSE
RAYSHUN SCOTT (USA)...188

ACKNOWLEDGEMENTS

We want to acknowledge every content contributor within the pages of this book. Each coauthor opened their heart, mind, spirit, and soul by getting their stories out of their head to be published and read. The Pathway To Trauma Recovery for each coauthor is different, yet the combined similarities have now come to light. The brave, authentic, impactful experience expressed by everyone is a guiding beacon of light with a mission to help and serve others.

Our mission is to Transform Pain Into Power, which will unlock the door and help others overcome the mystery of trauma from childhood, adolescence, and adulthood. This empowering group of writers dived deep into their stories and shared some painful moments of trials, tribulations, roadblocks, setbacks, forks in the road, and dead-end experiences.

From each experience came their transformational walk down the pathway of thriving, not just surviving. You will read about their challenges and, more importantly, their many successes, proving that life is not what happens to you; how you respond to it matters.
Sharing one's personal story is complex and takes you down memory lane. Each coauthor was willing to go back in time and open up about things that, in some instances, were never shared with anyone. However, they did not stay there. We acknowledge their ongoing empowering transformational success along their journey of self-discovery along the Pathway of Trauma Recovery. We thank you for your story and, more importantly, your leadership.

Wellness Coach Liz
Coach Michael Bart Mathews

TESTIMONIAL/PRAISE

Testimonial for Wellness Coach Liz (USA)

I fully endorse Wellness Coach Liz Blanding and her work in Trauma Awareness. I know her story, her amazing chapter in this book, and her podcast, "Get Trauma-Informed," will inspire, encourage, and motivate you to reignite your inner light and fulfill your purpose. Coach Liz did an amazing job delving into what people need to do on their Pathway To Trauma Recovery to get their lives back on track!

Marques Ogden (USA)
Former NFL Athlete
Owner Ogden Ventures, LLC

Testimonial for Coach Michael Bart Mathews (USA)

Michael Bart Mathews, the managing director and check-in coordinator, created this must-read book, "Pathway To Trauma Recovery," with all the coauthors and their literary contributions. This book is filled with heartwarming stories highlighting Trauma-Informed Awareness from surviving to thriving. The mission: Share with those suffering (in silence) because you are not alone! I am pleased to endorse Coach Michael Bart Mathews as an excellent International Speaker, Life Coach, Trauma Recovery Practitioner, Certified Addiction Recovery Coach, Manuscript Development Coach, and Award-Winning Author. Thank you, my dear friend!

Amy Sayama (USA)
Certified Integrated Health Coach
Certifications: Chopra Center, Laughter Yoga, Zen Bon Meditation

<u>**Testimonial for Beverly LaRue (USA)**</u>

I met Ms. Beverly LaRue several years ago while acting in a play written and directed by her colleague. Once the play was over, she approached me about an upcoming play she had written and was too direct. I kindly accepted the offer, and thus, our relationship was born. Ms. Beverly advocates for supporting Mental Health, Domestic Violence, and Trauma-related issues within some of her plays' storylines. This kind, God-fearing woman has a way with people that shines beyond the production stage. Ms. Beverly founded 4D-Productions, known for displaying the heart of drama within her creative talent in playwriting.

Kevin Morrow (USA)
Former Dean of Students at Hales Franciscan High School
Actor-Television Show/The Chi
Entrepreneur/Business Owner
Overseer of Abundance of Life Ministry
(Where wife Anita Morrow is Pastor)

<u>**Testimonial for Belinda Oosthuizen (SOUTH AFRICA)**</u>

I first met Belinda when I was speaking at a business conference in 2017. She had a light around her that exuberated a depth of warmth that you don't feel from many other people. Regardless of the troubles of her past, you knew she had survived a tremendous amount of trauma that helped Belinda thrive and become the person she is today. She is now able to empower others with her unwavering resilience and persistence using the power of her story.

Dan Woodruff (London)
International Speaker
Business Owner/Martial Arts Expert

<u>**Testimonial for Delphine Harris (USA)**</u>

Delphine Harris is a Powerhouse when it comes to the Spirit of God. She always acknowledges him, and He has directed her paths—Proverbs 3:5.

She has overcome many adversities in her life. She has triumphed over trauma, which makes her an ideal model to follow if you are in a season of challenges…not only will her story inspire you, but she sets a standard of overcoming and arising challenges she has faced.

She is the Founder and CEO of *I'm Doing Me, NOW LLC.* She exemplifies excellence in her field. As a Certified Image Consultant, I'm profoundly Blessed and honored that she calls me her Sister-in-Christ.

Ann Daschke (USA)

<u>**Testimonial for Kgabo Lucia Manthata (SOUTH AFRICA)**</u>

Kgabo Lucia Manthata is a resilient and formidable entrepreneur who has proven successful in all her business ventures. She is an inspirational entrepreneur and a highly impactful business coach and mentor. Kgabo Lucia Manthata has a never-say-die attitude, and she gets things done. Her strength and resilience are impeachable. No matter what life throws at her, she manages to bounce back stronger than before. She conquers all of her fears. I am proud to endorse Kgabo Lucia Manthata and her empowering chapter inside the pages of this must-read book.

Hetty, The Entrepreneur (South Africa)
South Africa's Number 1 Monetization Expert
Author of Monetize with Hetty The Entrepreneur

<u>**Testimonial for Rayshaun Scott (USA)**</u>

It's funny that even though we are brothers, we haven't known each other (all our lives). However, I have known Ray long enough to see his tremendous growth. His dedication and faithfulness to his family, friends, and career have shown me what can happen when a person finds God! His passion for helping and guiding our youth has shown me that there are still good people in this world.

Rob S (USA)
Robs 2 Cents
https://youtube.com/@robs2cents207?si=47mgJVSIVeHG9jDF

<u>**Testimonial for Timmy Young (USA)**</u>

I have been Blessed by Timmy's professional recommendations, loved by his wife and daughters, and strengthened in relationships because of the friendship he so freely shares. Timmy strives to serve his community and family through his unwavering faith and discipleship of Christ.

Timmy's story is one of resilience, faith, and boundless love. You will feel his warmth in the story he shares in his chapter. Through the joys and challenges of marriage to his beloved wife, Liz, and the Blessings of raising five children and welcoming five grandchildren, Timmy shares his wisdom from overcoming ordinary and trauma-related issues from his life experiences.

Rachael Melot, Author and Podcast host
The Ten Commandments of #SuccessWithoutApology
Rachael Monroe Melot (USA)
405.410.3554
VoteRachael.com

<u>**Testimonial for Tracy Whitt: (USA)**</u>

A principle of Christian ministry that stands the test of time is this: Someone who has been set free from something, healed and restored from something, is in a position to effectively minister to others facing the need for similar release and restoration. Tracy Whitt has herself been delivered, set free, from unhealthy patterns in her past and the trauma associated with them. She is uniquely equipped to help guide others along the pathway of release and recovery. She has answered the call to make this her mission in life for she knows the road to full recovery and longs to assist others in walking it. I have known Tracy for more than five years and witnessed her journey of grace-filled triumph over the hurt that once held her down. Her counsel and companionship in this publication will prove indispensable for anyone on the journey to wellness!

Warner Durnell (USA)
Presbyterian Pastor and Friend

FOREWORD

A group of phenomenal coauthors wrote this amazing book, Pathway to Trauma Recovery. Their heartfelt short stories offer a sneak peek into the overall good, bad, right, or wrong Pathway to Recovery from any exposure hidden secretly behind closed doors and kept silent for many years.

Like most empowering men and women who are brave enough, confident enough, and bold enough to throw their fear into the wind and tell their authentic and powerful stories, they change the lives of the masses. This is a powerful tool because everyone loves metaphors, and people love listening to a hero's journey.

Think about it. What movie was made in the 1970s, and here we are in the 2020s, and a version of this movie continues to show up in the box offices and crush sales, time and time again? Give up? Rocky! Rocky Balboa has been in movie theaters, on big screens, in our homes, and most importantly, in our hearts for almost six decades. Think about this: people worldwide have loved the movie Rocky for nearly sixty years, which made Sylvester Stallone a global sensation. That is the power of storytelling.

Let's take another great story, The Odyssey, written by Homer. This story has been told literally for centuries, and it is a classic tale of an individual facing extreme adversity and overcoming obstacles to get to a place of triumph and victory. This is what people love, and honestly, it is what people need to push forward in their lives. That is what The Pathway to Trauma Recovery book is all about. It is about energizing people and breathing inspiration into their minds, bodies, spirits, and souls to help them lead happy and fulfilled lives.

Pathway to Trauma Recovery is a book written to inspire, educate, and breathe life into people reading every amazing and inspirational story. All the coauthors did a fantastic job delving into what people need to do to get their lives back on track! One of the things that I have learned most of all in life, with many of the failures and mistakes I have made, is that no matter who you are or where you are in life, your story is never entirely written.

Your story is never truly finished unless you give up on yourselves or throw in the towel. I have been bankrupt, I have been broke, I have lost all my money. I have lost all my friends, I have had to start over from complete rock bottom, and I have had to dig myself out from the depths of hell to get myself back to a place of serenity, fulfillment, and prosperity.

It took me many years of my life to accomplish this achievement. I can say without hesitation that I never (ever) quit on myself, no matter how much adversity, darkness, and despair I had to overcome and or endure.

Assuming you are looking for a book that is going to tell you how to recover from hardship, despair, or darkness, this is the book for you! This book is full of great stories, actionable action steps, and all other information that will allow you to achieve your goal for yourself, whatever that might be! As an individual who struggled with addiction, overcoming darkness, and trying to push through adversity, this is an excellent read! I fully endorse this amazing book and know the stories will inspire the masses!

I write this foreword in the highest regards...

Marques Ogden (USA)
Former NFL Professional Athlete
Owner Ogden Ventures LLC

INTRODUCTION

Trauma is a fact of life. Everyone, regardless of whether you are Trauma-Informed or not, has experienced some trauma-related situations in their childhood, adolescence, or adult life cycle. Some have experienced Trauma during all three life cycles. Your Trauma may have come from physical abuse, sexual molestation, bullying, toxic relationships, death, abandonment, betrayal, adverse childhood experiences, neglect, medical abuse of power, cultural, systemic oppression, dysfunctional family dynamics, domestic violence, physical violence, mental abuse, alcohol and or drug addiction, or military experience.

Your Trauma-Informed experience may have come from witnessing someone else's Trauma-related experience, and you were powerless because of the nature of the circumstances.

Veterans, family members, and close friends of the family deal with the painful aftermath of the combat veteran's war-torn PTSD – Post Traumatic Stress Syndrome experience. Take PTSD, for example. One might experience any, if not all, of the following once triggered: flashbacks, memory lapses, distorted sense of self-worth, inability to control emotions, sleep disturbances, challenging interpersonal relationships with spouse, family, friends, and on occasion, with strangers, to name a few.

Complex PTSD or CPTSD: You stay stuck in the fight, flight, or freeze mode because, unbeknownst to you, your limbic system gets flooded with stress hormones. Emotional Trauma gets stuck in your body, and you react with any of the three mentioned above modalities, which are FIGHT, FLIGHT, AND FREEZE.

Stored Trauma, if not addressed, may show up in any of the following forms: insomnia, anxiety, dissociation, muscle tension, depression, anger, memory issues, difficulty communicating, avoidance coping, back pain, nightmares, brain fog, exhaustion, headaches, low energy, aches, pains, diarrhea, constipation, and nausea to name a few ways stored Trauma rears its ugly head.

One of the most widespread forms of Trauma is sexual abuse. According to the National Association of Adult Survivors of Child Abuse, there are more than 42 million survivors of sexual abuse in America. Furthermore, according to the National Children's Alliance and the Advocacy Center, one in three girls and one in five boys are sexually abused before the age of eighteen. One in five children are solicited sexually while on the internet before the age of eighteen.

Those statistics are staggering; therefore, it is safe to say that either you or someone that you know has been molested and or grew up with alcoholics. It is almost a certainty you or someone that you know (married or single) have experienced physical violence, either being the perpetrator or the victim.

Becoming Trauma-Informed is The Pathway To Recovery and is essential to understanding trauma survivors. This is not just another book to be read and placed on the shelf. It is a blueprint, a journey to deep healing and restoration. Woven on the pages of this collaborative work, you will meet some of the most courageous authors from around the world, knitted together by a single thread: the thread of Trauma. Our content contributors live in the beautiful countries of South Africa, the Netherlands, Lebanon, the United Kingdom, and several states within the United States.

Through the common thread of Trauma and the required self-work of recovery and realignment, the authors unmask and let you into their (personal) journeys of healing. Trauma does not discriminate, and it is not a respecter of a person. Trauma can strike anyone by the mere proximity of an event or person on a warpath.

Each coauthor sharing their experience highlights how Trauma affects people worldwide. Psychological and physical Trauma are inseparable from its lasting effects on people. Mindset plays a vital role in Trauma recovery. The physical aspects can leave visual scars that can have long-lasting mental and psychological impacts on one's thinking and trusting others.

OUR WRITERS CONSIST OF:

One Doctor of Theology Degree, two Doctors in Divinity Degrees, one Naturopathic Wellness Coach, two Certified Trauma

Recovery Practitioners, three Certified Life Coaches, three (CARC) Certified Addiction Recovery Coaches, Certified Abuse Recovery Coaches, Four Spiritual Counselors, and Five Ministers who all are trauma survivors, and contributing coauthors in this book. We believe there is a spiritual base to healing the hurt. It would help if you decided for yourself based on completing your due diligence.

We took the time to earn our certifications, which have allowed us to deal with our past by becoming aware and Trauma-Informed. As experts in Trauma education, we are better equipped to aid, assist, and coach you throughout your Trauma journey as you find your moment of clarity by seeking your power within.

For those who believe in their Higher Power (regardless of their religious beliefs), there is an energy source, a power source greater than you and me. Positive affirmations and prayer to their Higher Power are indispensable sources of empowerment, faith, hope, and transformation.

Our Trauma-related storylines were thoughtfully crafted deep down in each coauthor's mind, body, spirit, and soul. Our mission is to contribute to this amazing Pathway To Trauma Recovery Journey.

Every coauthor not only talked the talk, but we also walked the walk by experiencing many Trauma-related subjects between us. Our authentic, real-life confessions are proof-positive testimonials of "been there, done that." Now, it's time to heal the hurt.

Being Trauma-Informed welcomes self-determination, empowerment, and transformation in Trauma-related experiences, not limited to PTSD (as mentioned above), dissociation, addiction, treatment, mindfulness, self-care, and relapse prevention along your recovery journey.

Learning and understanding the differences between being Trauma-Informed and the effect of unresolved Trauma is a critical start to your healing process. You can move past the victim/survivor mentality to become the bright, shining, illuminating beacon of faith, hope, and transformation to thrive and live your best life.

When you change the way you look at Trauma, the Trauma you look at changes. Look at Trauma as not being your fault. You do not need to carry around the 100-pound baggage blocker on your back that is filled with heavy, and we do mean heavy trauma-related issues that you may or may not have addressed.

You can find answers inside the pages of this book, Pathway To Trauma Recovery. We let the cat out of the bag. We are not hiding in the closet of guilt or shame because there is no need to. We are not suffering in silence as millions of others choose to do so. We are an open book filled with story after life-changing story that depicts our past, does not define our present, and looks into our purpose-driven future.

Wellness Coach Liz Blanding
Coach Michael Bart Mathews

CHAPTER ONE
A FAMILY SECRET - THE IMPACT OF UNRESOLVED TRAUMA
WELLNESS COACH LIZ BLANDING (USA)

This chapter delves into my complex and emotional life's journey, marked by family secrets, trauma, and the pursuit of recovery and transformation. It touches upon themes of abuse, identity, relationships, and the resilience of the human spirit.

I share a powerful narrative of my experiences, including witnessing a traumatic event as a child, growing up with a family secret, and the emotional impact of such hidden truths. It also highlights the importance of self-discovery and personal growth in overcoming adversity.

While planning a funeral for a man I barely knew, I felt numbness and confusion. The deceased, James, was rumored to be my Father, but I had little connection with him. Two weeks after his passing, my younger sister and I faced the responsibility of settling his affairs.

As we unraveled James's life, we discovered a web of secrets. The family's stories of our upbringing no longer made sense. Driven by curiosity, I started questioning the narratives that had shaped my life.

I was told my biological Father was an abusive man named James, who terrorized my mother during their marriage. My mother married James when she was just 18, escaping her own abusive mother's home. The marriage quickly turned into a nightmare of violence and suffering. The abuse continued even during her pregnancy with me.

Research suggests that trauma experienced by a pregnant mother can affect the unborn child's development. High levels of stress and the hormone cortisol can harm the baby's brain and emotional development, potentially leading to difficulties in managing emotions and forming healthy relationships later in life.

My early memories were blurred, but one horrifying incident remained vivid in my mind. At the age of three, I witnessed James stabbing my mother repeatedly, leaving both myself and my baby sister traumatized. The effects of this traumatic event were profound, and although there were no physical injuries, the emotional scars remained unaddressed.

Doctors explained that my mother had survived the attack by mere inches, but James was never arrested or charged, leaving the family in constant fear. The whispers and secrecy within the family only added to my feelings of deception, insecurity, and fear. I knew a deep family secret existed but was the last to discover it.

As I grew up in a family marked by violence and substance abuse, I developed low self-esteem and struggled to form healthy relationships. My stepfather, while providing for the family, failed to protect me from emotional abuse, including demeaning jokes about my weight.

A father's role is to protect and guide his daughter, but my experience was far from ideal. I carried the weight of emotional baggage into adulthood, affecting my self-esteem and relationships. The family secret exacerbated my feelings of confusion and isolation.

It wasn't until later in life that I began my transformation. I realized that I had the power to recover and thrive, and I refused to be defined by my traumatic past.

I studied and formed an understanding of the Effects of Unresolved Trauma through Erikson's Theory:

Eric Erikson's theory of psychosocial development highlights the importance of early experiences in shaping an individual's identity and ability to form healthy relationships. Traumatic events during childhood (such as witnessing violence or experiencing emotional abuse) can significantly impact a person's development.

In my case, the trauma I witnessed at a young age left deep emotional scars, affecting my self-esteem, relationships, and decision-making. Erikson's theory emphasizes the need for positive experiences and supportive relationships during each stage of development. When trauma disrupts these stages, individuals may struggle to achieve healthy psychosocial development.

My journey illustrates the devastating effects of unresolved trauma and family secrets on a person's life. My transformation and pursuit of realignment and recovery serve as a testament to the resilience of the human spirit. Erikson's theory provides insight into the lasting impact of early trauma, emphasizing the importance of addressing and recovering from such experiences to achieve healthy psychosocial development.

Early Childhood (Infancy to 18 Months): Trust vs. Mistrust

In infancy, a child learns to trust their caregivers. They rely on their parents or caregivers to provide for their physical and emotional needs. In my case, my early experiences were marked by fear and instability due to my mother's abusive marriage. The trauma I witnessed during this period instilled mistrust and fear in my developing psyche.

Early Childhood (18 Months to 3 Years): Autonomy vs. Shame and Doubt

During this stage, children start to explore their independence. They begin to assert themselves and make choices. For me, the trauma I witnessed at the age of three, when James repeatedly stabbed my mother, had a profound impact on my developing sense of autonomy. The fear and helplessness I felt during this traumatic event led to feelings of shame and doubt about my ability to control my environment.

Preschool (3 to 5 Years): Initiative vs. Guilt

In preschool, children start to take initiative in their activities and develop a sense of purpose. However, unresolved trauma can lead to a sense of guilt and fear of taking initiative. My traumatic early experiences hindered my ability to understand that I was good enough. While exploring my interests and developing a sense of purpose is healthy, I became a workaholic. Any activity pursued with extreme disregard for healthy balance is an addiction and can have devastating consequences when left unbalanced, misaligned, and untreated.

School Age (6 to 11 Years): Industry vs. Inferiority

During this stage, children learn to be competent and productive. They develop skills and seek approval from authority figures. In my case, the ongoing trauma and emotional abuse within my family contributed to feelings of inferiority and a lack of self-confidence. I have struggled and pressed hard to excel academically and socially due to the unresolved trauma I carried.

Adolescence (12 to 18 Years): Identity vs. Role Confusion

Individuals explore their adolescent identity and strive to establish a sense of self. They navigate the challenges of peer relationships and self-discovery. For me, the impact of my traumatic childhood continued to affect my self-esteem and relationships during this crucial stage of development. I have grappled with identity issues and difficulty forming healthy connections with others, especially those who had mis-intent in their hearts and deeds.

As I continued my studies, I developed an understanding of the Generational Impact of Trauma.

I further began to understand why I saw life through a different lens and how unresolved trauma had a generational impact on my family. Trauma passed down from one generation to the next can perpetuate cycles of abuse, dysfunction, and emotional distress. Breaking these cycles through awareness, recovery, realignment, and support is essential.

BOOM!!!BANG!!!CRASH!!!SCREAMS!!! Yes, did you feel it? What just happened? We were talking about support, awareness, and breaking cycles. Wait, I'm confused. Yes, **life happens, and it's** just like that. A sudden shift is just where my story took me. I hit a brick wall. It was a tree at the top of an expressway embankment. One icy, snowy morning in rush hour traffic, a car hydroplanes into my truck, flinging me and my mother three lanes over and up into a tree at street level. When I regained consciousness, my head was smashed into the airbag. I looked over at my mother, and she was not moving. One of her legs was hanging out the door. I jumped out of the truck wearing high-heeled boots and walked behind my vehicle, which was on an incline, to reach the other side to help my mother. When I reached her, she asked me if I thought the truck was going to roll backward. I looked down at the gear shift, which was still in drive. I snatched my mother to the ground. The tree's grip on the truck loosened a split second later; my truck rolled backward, down onto the expressway. The speeding traffic hit and totaled my truck.

There we were at the top of the hill, my mother crying her eyes out, yelling and screaming, Lord, we can't take anymore. I jumped up and down, vomited air and stomach fluid, and thanked God for saving us. We were in traffic that morning going to probate court to gain guardianship over my stepfather, who had been slipping into the darkness of dementia for the past ten years. We had recently buried upward of ten close family members. Now we, the backbone of the family, are sitting on the side of a snow and ice-covered hilltop. It was a cold winter morning, and we were unaware of the pain that followed the bang-up that we survived.

We watched the emergency responders, police officers, and tow truck drivers clear the accident. Then, the police officers had to figure out how to get us down from the top of the hill to get medical attention. A fence separated the grass and trees from the pedestrian side of the street.

After waking up a few days later, when the adrenaline rush wore off, my body was in excruciating pain. As time went on, I endured every type of therapy, including occupational therapy, physical therapy, psychotherapy, and manipulation under anesthesia, to regain mobility in my body and limbs.

Doctor after doctor, specialist after specialist, told me I had plateaued and would not get any better. **Finally, I knew it was time to work on myself. I refused to believe that it was all over for me. I was a single, divorced mom with too much to accomplish. My children needed me to get better. I remember repeating aloud to my doctors, myself, and anyone willing to listen: My current situation is not my destiny. My transformation began!**

God had shown me more about my purpose and life than the prognosis the doctors wanted me to accept. I refused to believe that I would be wheelchair-bound if I did not have double knee replacement surgery. I refused to think that I would ever be able to regain a thriving lifestyle ever again. No, I was not hearing it. I went to work. Traditional medical professionals told me that I would not get any better if I did not accept where I was. I remember telling myself that I would not get any better if I accepted what the doctors told me.

As I was sitting at home watching the replay of my truck rolling back down into traffic and after being saved from a horrific car accident like that one, it was time to get a grip and stop repeating the same mistakes over and over again in my life's journey. It was time to realize that no one was coming to save me! No one was coming to make me feel safe! No one was going to save me but me and my faith in God! I had to protect the little girl inside of myself. I had to thrive and not just survive. So, I surrendered my victim mentality, gave up my survivor title, and exchanged it for a badge of honor as a THRIVER!

When pivoting from pain to gain, there must be a shift. I am a literal, visual person. For me, a transformation or change may look a little drastic to someone else; however, this is my story to write and tell. I was born Mary Elizabeth Coston. However beautiful for some, that name represents a lifetime of tremendous, unbearable pain for me. For me to shift from pain to power, it took something drastic. It took something that would remind me, my inner adult, daily to stand up for that little girl, my inner child, who was never protected. It took me to draw a line (you know), like the circle with the bright red line standing for no more of this or that. The name change from Mary to Liz was what it took for me to pivot.

My Adulthood: Recovery, Realignment and Transformation

Despite the profound effects of my traumatic childhood coupled with a devastating car accident, my journey is one of recovery, realignment, and transformation. I refused to let my past define me, and through faith, natural medicine, trauma recovery, and self-discovery, I embarked on a path of recovery, realignment, and self-empowerment. I also recognized the generational impact of family secrets and the physical and psychological devastating anguish of unresolved trauma. I sought to break the cycle and embarked on a **PATH TO RECOVERY** and self-empowerment.

After my accident, I faced a daunting recovery process. The traditional medical approach suggested the use of medications, surgeries, and treatments that were invasive and, frankly, terrifying to me. This fear was the spark that ignited my search for alternative methods. I was convinced there had to be a better way to recover without resorting to potentially harmful treatments. My exploration led me to the world of naturopathic medicine and trauma recovery, where I found solace and efficacy in natural remedies and holistic practices. This journey wasn't just about finding alternatives and rediscovering the ancient wisdom that respects and harnesses the body's natural recovery capabilities.

During my recovery and daily practice of realignment, I learned to listen deeply to my body. Each pain and discomfort told a story, guiding me toward recovery and teaching me the language of my well-being. Patience and persistence became my allies. I realized recovery is a gradual process filled with small achievements and occasional setbacks. It taught me the importance of celebrating every step forward and maintaining hope.

I also learned the value of community. The support and love from my family, friends, and even strangers were invaluable. They reminded me that recovery is a collective journey, not a solitary one. This realization became a fundamental principle in my academy, where we foster a supportive and nurturing environment.

Perhaps the most transformative aspect of my journey was discovering my inner strength. In moments of weakness, I found a resilience I never knew I had. This newfound strength didn't just fuel my recovery; it propelled me into new ventures as an author and entrepreneur. Please understand that recovery and realignment is a daily commitment. It is not, let me repeat, it is not a one and done situation. It is a commitment to daily self-care. Relapse is real and hits very hard. The light at the end of the tunnel of trauma for me was and is my faith, constantly building resiliency by following my program and a healthy holistic support system.

This is why I created the eight-week Resilient Entrepreneurs Group Coaching program. The Total Mind-Body Realignment, Post Trauma program allows Entrepreneurs and Business Owners to work through their unresolved traumas, creating a better performance in their personal lives and businesses. While my flagship program is focused on Business Owners, the self-care and resilience-building techniques work for anyone suffering in silence from unresolved trauma.

The program was just what I needed to discover the physiological trauma that began to manifest in my physical body in addition to the physical trauma stored in my cells from past trauma, i.e., the car accident. While non-traditional, the herbs, the different modalities, the breath work, deep stretching, and various practices and techniques spoke to the very fiber of my being. Coupled with building a supportive network and community of others who understood my journey, a winning formula was born.

A program designed for post-trauma 'Thrivers' supporting post-trauma 'Survivors' to become Thrivers. Wait for it!!! Did you catch that? Go back and reread that statement. How powerful! I just saw an advertisement for e-harmony online dating, and the tagline for the ad was meeting people get you. That did it for me. How amazing is it not to be judged for having gone through traumatic experiences that left you with confusion, numbness, and uncertainty but to be a part of a community that offers support and reassurance that hope and help is available? That a life without constant fear and doubt is also available. **Simple, Amazing!**

Yes, this is what the Oasis Wellness Centers have to offer—a community and support designed just for you. No, I will not give false hope that you will wake up one morning and the horrible trauma-induced feelings magically disappear. However, I will say that each day is much better when you are equipped with the right tools, self-care plans, strategies, intentional focus, and healthy support. When we are equipped with resources, we have the power to create a better life, recovering and realigning from the trauma residue of PTSD, Anxiety, Depression, Insolation, Loneliness, Insomnia, Worry, Fear, and a plethora of debilitating symptoms. We take back control of our lives, and that is worth everything.

I am known as **"The Breakthrough Specialist and Soother," which** reflects my commitment to guiding individuals through their transformative journeys. My certifications in Naturopathic Medicine, Trauma Recovery Coaching, and Addiction/Abuse Recovery Coaching enable me to offer comprehensive support, workshops, retreats, and realignment programs that support a healthy holistic journey to a life where you will be equipped with the tools and techniques of resiliency and the ability to Thrive.

I view coaching others into transformation and purpose as my ministry. We solve the problem of trauma recovery and realignment for those seeking active participation in their holistic health education and recovery journey. My team and I work collaboratively to provide accessible, holistic wellness options. What sets us apart is not just our expertise but our personal experiences in recovery and realignment, our heartfelt desire to assist others, and our ability to create a community centered around holistic wellness.

In this world, we create what we need. I am the founder of Oasis Wellness Centers, which offers a wide range of services and products aligned with holistic health principles. Under the umbrella of the wellness center, we house an academy, which is a cornerstone of our offerings, where we educate on the historical uses of herbs, their properties, and their impact on the body, drawing inspiration from Hippocrates' philosophy of 'Let thy food be thy medicine.' This approach is also biblically supported, acknowledging the natural recovery power of herbs. Additionally, I developed a product, the 'Soothing Salve,' a blend of over 30 natural herbs designed to aid in circulation, pain management, and reducing swelling, among other benefits.

My mission is to provide holistic solutions that address the physical and psychological aspects of health. My inspiration and heartfelt desire behind my work are knowing that what has worked for me can work and be a blessing to others, seeking alternative natural options for overcoming health challenges, body maintenance, realignment, and recovery.

While I'm proud of my professional achievements, my greatest pride lies in my family – my children and grandchildren. Building and living a legacy with them, grounded in the belief that 'nothing is too hard for God,' is immensely fulfilling.

I'm also proud of the growing community we're nurturing, which is spreading education and awareness in the holistic industry. This community is based on authenticity, integrity, and a genuine desire to help others. Our mantra, 'Relieving Pain, Creating Better Performance,' stems from my belief that sharing my story highlights the purpose of my pain – not only for my recovery but to provide real solutions and relief to others. My story is a testament of turning adversity into opportunity and pain into a legacy of recovery, realignment, self-discovery, and empowerment.

It is my desire to help others Break the Chains of Unresolved Trauma.

This part of my story is a powerful example of resilience and transformation. I highlighted the generational impact of trauma and the potential for recovery, realignment, and breaking free from the chains of the past. As I continue my devoted studies and practice in Holistic Trauma Recovery work, we'll uncover more layers of this compelling narrative, shedding light on the complexities of trauma and the human capacity for recovery, realignment, rebalancing, growth, and change.

My story is also a testament to the resilience of the human spirit and how faith works miracles. By sharing my story and insights, I offer hope and inspiration to you who may be on a similar path of recovery, realignment, and self-discovery. I want to leave you with lessons marked by personal challenges and significant triumphs, hoping you will find added value. Contact me for discovery and support because you are not alone. Help is available.

Here is what I learned:

1. **Resilience in the Face of Adversity**: My experience demonstrates the power of resilience. After a traumatic car accident and life-changing injuries, I didn't succumb to despair but instead sought alternative holistic paths to recovery.
2. **The Value of Alternative Medicine**: I turned towards naturopathic and holistic practices, highlighting the importance of considering alternative holistic medical approaches. This can be a crucial lesson for those seeking to learn more about their holistic options and choices.
3. **Empowerment through Education**: Opening a naturopathic academy not only empowers me, but also offers others the same education and self-determining powerful choices. Education and sharing knowledge, especially regarding health and wellness, is very important to me.
4. **Entrepreneurial Spirit**: My transition from real estate to becoming a best-selling author and holistic product creator exemplifies the entrepreneurial spirit. It underscores the idea that starting a new venture or following your passion is never too late.
5. **The Profound Impact of Personal Experiences on Professional Success:** My personal experiences deeply influence my professional life. I learned that personal challenges can be transformed into professional triumphs.
6. **Community Building:** I am building a community of individuals and experts with similar interests and challenges by creating products and an academy. Community is crucial in recovery, realignment, and personal growth.
7. **Lifelong Learning and Adaptability**: I am committed to lifelong learning and adaptability. Embracing new knowledge and skills at any stage of life can lead to unexpected and fulfilling paths.
8. **The Power of Sharing One's Story**: As a best-selling author, I share my story, which I have been told has been helpful to others. It is my prayer that my story be therapeutic and inspirational for others. It shows the

power of storytelling in recovery, realignment, and motivating others.

9. **Balance in Life**: Again, I pray that juggling personal challenges, a career shift, disabilities, and family responsibilities (as a mother and grandmother) will demonstrate the importance of balance in life and what is possible. I must quote the amazing Lisa Nichols, a beacon of resiliency and strength: "Winners never Quit, and Quitters never Win."

10. **The Importance of Self-Care:** I turned to holistic practices, which underline the significance of physical and mental self-care, which is crucial for my overall well-being.

There is power in perseverance, value in holistic alternative paths, and the impact one person can have by turning their struggles into a source of strength and inspiration for others. Here is to your recovery and realignment post-trauma.

A Special Note:

Heartbroken Daddy-Less Daughters - A Breeding Ground for Trauma

The daddy-less daughter issues in our family began when my great-grandfather was lynched. My great-grandmother (his wife) and children were forced off his land. This created a generation of daddy-less daughters. Why? I'm glad you asked. When a father's influence and love are absent from a daughter's life, her "Picker," meaning her ability to select a proper mate, is skewed by the need & desire to anesthetize her present pain. Generation after generation of women in our family have used love as a drug to feel good. We learned by exposure that we had no other choice. So, daughters' I am here to let you know you have choices. A choice to be with a man who will love you, care for you, protect you, cover you, and grow with you.

Throughout the many adversities surrounding my story, I knew I was destined to find my seeds of greatness. May you find your seeds of greatness within my story. Remember, you are not alone.

If I can thrive, not just survive, so can you. **JOIN OUR COMMUNITY TODAY**. Become a Thriver!!!

– Liz Blanding, Holistic Recovery Coach

Wellness Coach Liz Blanding has helped people come out of the shadows and regain their strength because, coming from her grandson, (Me), Jaydin, I have known that no matter what, my grandmother will push herself as a great leader – **Jaydin Blanding.**

My loving, heartfelt testimony to you, GIRL! Inspiring…Encouraging…Motivational…Life Coach? How has my mother NOT been each and every one of these things for me? That is the real question. My mother inspires me every time she gets out of bed in the morning and keeps going. Knowing where she has been and what she has been through. My mother has been encouraging me ever since I've been in her womb. Every day of her pregnancy was a test of her strength and resilience. Being a mother to twins, I know exactly what a journey it is to give life to 2! Just knowing she was in my (same) shoes and how similar we both are, and she is still pushing with purpose, motivates my every breath. She has coached my life in ways neither of us probably even knew! To this day, the way I move, the way I think, my strength and my perseverance are all direct reflections of my mother. Her love and legacy will forever live through me.

Tatyana Duskin

ABOUT THE AUTHOR

LIZ BLANDING

HOLISTIC RECOVERY COACH, BEST-SELLING AUTHOR, NATUROPATHIC WELLNESS COACH

Wellness Coach Liz Blanding is a business owner driven by her passion for empowering and educating others in the arena of Natural Wellness. She is the Founder and C.E.O. of Oasis Wellness Centers, an online holistic herbal wellness academy. She is the Founder of Soothing Salve, an organic herbal blend of over 30 herbs designed to relieve aches and pains from joints, sore, tight muscles and inflammation.

She is the published author of "IT'S SMOOTHIE TIME," a fun book to kick start your journey into making healthier nutritional choices that are mouth-watering and full of flavor. She is the Lead Author of "The Pathway to Recovery " book. The book is a collaborative work where you meet fourteen courageous authors from around the world knitted together by a double thread which is the thread of Trauma and Recovery.

Coach Liz is a Brand Partner with Lifewave. A phenomenal company with patent phototherapy technology for performance enhancement. In addition, she became business partners with the phenomenal Coach Michael Bart Mathews. Together, they created F.Y.M.O.C - the Finding Your Moment of Clarity transformational system. F.Y.M.O.C teaches entrepreneurs business principles.

Coach Liz is a sought-after speaker, teacher, coach, talk show host, and content creator of two Podcasts, "Oasis Wellness of Life" on YouTube, and "Get Trauma Informed" found on Apple Podcast, Spotify, Amazon Music, iHeart Radio and YouTube Podcasting.

Her most prized titles are that of a Mom of three beautiful adult children, two additional sons by marriage, and nine amazing grandchildren. Yes, she is a Grandma, aka Buca, aka Nana.

Coach Liz has mentored, coached, and encouraged those in her circle to be the absolute best for many years. She learned the key to change was to mend her brokenness. For many years, deep down in her heart, Coach Liz knew her story was not meant for her suffering. The pain she suffered from childhood trauma and a debilitating car accident was not in vain! Her pain was not just for her to learn valuable lessons and grow from them. She needed to learn to develop and transform into today's intentional, purposeful woman. Her pain was and is for the thousands of survivors that suffered multiple traumas in loneliness and silence. Her life's mission is to extend an olive branch to those who have a deep desire to come out of the shadows of trauma and to walk into the light of thriving. Yes, it is possible to go from Surviving to Thriving. For this reason, Wellness Coach Liz Blanding is leading the Get Trauma Informed Movement.

Wellness Coach Liz Blanding:
Links to all socials: https://linktr.ee/dlblanding
Podcast: https://gettraumainformed.buzzsprout.com
Website: https://oasiswellnessctrs.com
Lifewave: https://www.lifewave.com/oasiswellnesscenters
Schedule your support appointment:
https://calendly.com/oasiswellnesscentersandacademy

CHAPTER TWO
HOW TO WIN IN THE GAME OF LIFE
MICHAEL BART MATHEWS (USA)

<u>MY CHILDHOOD STORY</u>

As I reflect on my childhood, up to age 11, growing up in the 1960s and '70s, we had access to everything: good, bad, right, and wrong, we had access. Streetology was a necessary must to survive. Surviving in Chicago during my childhood, adolescence, and adult life has yielded multiple traumatic blasts from my past. From running policies (the neighborhood lottery) to selling dinners to selling drugs, you could get what you wanted. Chicago bolstered some of the biggest gangs in America, and as sure as I am writing this chapter, back in the day, we could not escape gang activity. No, my neighborhood never joined the gangs, thanks to the older community members who protected us and kept the gangs at bay.

We traveled through gang territory to and from high school. Some faced bullying and public ridicule because they were unpopular or not in the 'In crowd.' Our parents had no idea about the level of stress, trauma, disruption, and uncertainty we faced outside of our community. They were too busy paying the bills, keeping clothes on our backs, and food on the table.

On the business side, Black-owned businesses were throughout my neighborhood. If my memory serves me correctly, within a five-minute radius of my house, the community resources included three churches, four corner stores, one fire department, three elementary schools, one concrete outdoor basketball court, one tavern, and two tool factories. As of 2024, the three elementary schools and churches are the only community resources remaining from my elementary through high school years. There is also a multimillion-dollar public library and a multimillion-dollar community center. Those two resources were unavailable when I was growing up. OMG, what if?

The authority figures growing up in an all-Black neighborhood (outside of the adults in my community) were white. The police officers, firefighters, school teachers, news reporters, insurance men, delivery drivers, City Bus Drivers, Doctors, and Nurses were all white. Yes, I saw a few Black teachers, and all the Preachers were Black; however, without any discriminatory intent, outside of the Black Business Owners and

Black Fathers, white men held the positions of authority. Sometimes, that authority caused traumatic experiences because they felt empowered to say things and do things that were derogatory in the eyes of my young mind.

During my childhood, between the ages of 8 and 11, my Father would pack up the car, and my Mother would fry a basket full of fried chicken, bread, cakes, cookies, chips, and water. Off we went down South to visit my Mother's and Father's side of the family.

My Mother and Auntie left the South in their early teens by catching a Greyhound Bus during the great migration North to Chicago. They told me stories filled with trauma-related issues that I never forgot about, including my Mom's experience with picking cotton in the hot sun all day, every day as a child. My Mother told me that she prayed to God that she didn't have to raise any children in the South. No, she was not pregnant when she said it. I knew my Grandpa and Grandma on my Mother's side; however, I only knew my Grandma on my Father's side. I remember the stories about my Grandpa on my Father's side that were passed down to me from my Father and my cousins.

My Father and my Uncles were subjected to Jim Crow dictatorship while growing up in the South, which caused my Father to join the great migration North across the Mason-Dixion Line in his early twenties. My Father and Mother met in Chicago, got married, and had three children, with me being the youngest.

Back to the story:

We stopped for gas after crossing into southern Illinois, close to the Missouri Border, in what we considered a small town. Remember, we were born and raised North in Chicago and had never been exposed to white-only and colored-only public restrooms. My older sister ran out of the car and raced toward the white-only restroom. Four to Five white men were sitting in front of the gas station, openly carrying shotguns and rifles. They stood up before my sister could touch the doorknob in the white-only restroom; my Mother grabbed her and stopped her in her tracks.

The white men sat down as my Mother and sister hurried to use the color-only restroom. My Father was watching as he continued pumping gas.

Afterward, he took my brother and me to the colored-only restroom after paying for the gas, and we drove off with no incident.

As we continued our journey deeper into the South, my parents gave us a verbal lesson on racism, segregation, and discrimination, which included our recent traumatic experience back at the gas station.

F.Y.I.: The above section of my chapter is not about racism or hate; it's about the traumatic outcome that many baby boomers may be suffering in silence who experienced some of my journeys, to some degree, during their childhood.

MY ADOLESCENT STORY:

As I reflect on my adolescent years, between the ages of 12 and 18, I will share another experience with a trauma-related situation that has stayed with me over the years.

I was not mature enough to listen to my inner guiding system, that man who sits on your shoulder and suggests that you do or don't do this or that. Some call it intuition, 'sixth sense,' or simply acting upon your comfortable feelings when things are right. Or not acting on your uncomfortable feelings when things feel wrong.

Allow me to take you on a journey that leads to a moment in time that will forever be with me.

I was a high school student-athlete, playing on the varsity basketball team as the starting center. I was around 16 years old, and I had a wonderful girlfriend. I'll call her Mickey. I was good friends with Mickey's cousin, who attended high school with me. One day, Mickey came to visit her cousin, and we met. From then on, it was Mickey and me, hand in hand.

Mickey would visit her cousin, and that's where we would meet. We would do things teenagers did. Mickey lived in the Chicago Housing Projects. I'm not knocking the families and some of my friends who lived in the projects; I'm simply highlighting that if you did not live in the projects and came to visit someone, everyone knew you didn't belong. That was the case with me.

Our basketball team was a contender in my senior year for the Illinois Class A.A. Boys High School State Championship. Mickey would occasionally tell me that her Mother wanted to meet me. And would I come to see her? Remember, Mickey's family lived in the projects; I had never been in her building. Whenever Mickey asked me to go and meet her Mother, I felt uncomfortable inside. My inner guiding system made me feel uneasy about making the trip. It was not about FEAR; it was about having enough Streetology to know where and where not to go.

On that fateful day, Mickey asked me again to meet her Mother. She would show her newspaper clippings of our basketball team as we won game after game. Her Mother wanted to meet me to gauge our intentions.

It was time for our team to play in the City of Chicago, Class A.A. High School Basketball City Championship Game. The newspapers, radio, and television stations covered the game big time, and Mickey continued sharing our basketball success with her Mother. Against my feelings from my inner guiding system, institution, and Streetology, I decided it would not hurt to make one visit, meet Mickey's Mother and family, and leave quietly.

I asked my Father if I could drive his car, and for the first time during my high school days, my Dad said yes. Mickey and I went to visit her family, especially her Mother. We arrived at her building (Chicago Public Housing Project) on State Street in Chicago, parked, and entered the building. About eight to ten youngsters stood out front as we approached the elevators. They all said hello, Mickey. I felt better because I thought these were her friends and we were all good. They did not verbally speak to me. However, they gave me the customary head nod, and I returned (the nod) without saying a word.

We rode the elevator to the 14th floor, which stopped on every floor. Every time the door opened, I got strange looks from the people getting on and off because they knew I did live there. They all knew and spoke to Mickey. For the second time, I felt we would all be okay. We got off the elevator. Mickey used her key to open the door, and her Mother sat on the couch with a big smile. She stands up, walks over to me, gives me a long, tight hug, and says, it's so lovely to meet you.

Her family comes out, and we exchange pleasantries over a home-cooked meal. By now, my inhibitions of uncomfortable inner feelings were completely gone. Mickey's family welcomed me with open arms.

It was getting late, and I had to have my Dad's car back at a specific time, and I did not want to mess up. We said our goodbyes, rode the elevator to the ground floor, and exited the building. Unbeknownst to me, the guys in front of the building, who had spoken to Mickey when we had come in, were still there, as if they were waiting for us to leave.

Without warning, several of the guys pulled out guns, and one of the guys put a gun up to my head and told me not to move. As he went through my pockets, they told Mickey she better not say anything and we better not call the police. Don't forget, Mickey, your family lives in this building, and you do not want anything to happen to them, do you? They took the little money I had in my pockets and my Dad's car keys. They took Mickey's purse, and one of the guys emptied it and took what little money she had. Remember, the robbers called Mickey by name because they lived in the same building.

I asked them if I could have my Dad's car keys back. One of the guys threw the keys and hit me in the chest. I could feel the pain because my Dad had a large ring full of keys. I was worried about Mickey and me getting shot during the entire time because the robbers looked like elementary school-age children, and they all had handguns.

Suddenly, a guardian angel appeared out of nowhere. An older man (a stranger) saw what was happening and began shooting up in the air to scare the robbers away. Unfortunately, as the robbers ran away, they turned around and shot at me and Mickey. I could hear bullets bouncing off the brick building and sparks flying upon impact. Writing this narrative reminded me of how I pushed Mickey to the ground, trying to escape harm's way. I did not think; I reacted based on instinct.

After the robbers were gone, I noticed my girlfriend, Mickey, had been shot in the leg. I was out of my mind. Blood was everywhere, Mickey was crying, she was in pain, and I was in a strange neighborhood. The Guardian Angel (That older man) helped me put Mickey into the back seat of my Dad's car and told me to drive her to Provident Hospital on 51st. On the way to the hospital, Mickey was still crying from the pain. I was nervous and sped until I arrived at the emergency room. I shouted to a couple of hospital personnel wearing scrubs that my girlfriend had been shot and needed medical attention. They took her out of the back seat, put her on a gurney, and rushed her into the emergency room after examining her wound. I did not know if Mickey was going to live or die. I nervously walked up and down the hallway, not knowing what else to do. I was all alone, 16 years old. I remember breaking out into a cold sweat.

While at the hospital, the doctors took care of Mickey's wound, and thank God it was not life-threatening. The doctors came out and gave me the good news. Two detectives showed up at the hospital and told us we had to come down to the police station to look at mug shots and try to identify the gunmen.

Mickey begged me not to point them out, even if I recognized them, because of the threat of harm the robbers promised to inflict on her family. While looking at the mugshots, I can honestly say that I did not recognize them. I do not know what I would have done if I had. Because of the trauma of getting a gun pointed at my head, getting robbed and shot at, and my girlfriend getting shot, my mind, body, spirit, and soul were off balance.

My inner child went into fear mode because I did not understand what had just happened. My adolescent self went into a rage, and I acted in the flight mode of survival. I did not have time to freeze, and I had nothing to fight back with because I did not carry a gun. I chose flight because it was my best option to get Mickey to the hospital as soon as possible. I thought nothing like an adult, even though my thought process was for Mickey's health and safety, as well as my own.

At age 16, I could not have explained this to you calmly. However, because today, I am a Certified Addiction Recovery Coach with Trauma-related training, I looked back into my life to understand the effect that trauma had on me. As you continue reading my story, if you are suffering in silence from a trauma-related past or present experience, there is help for you. You are not alone.

Now, back to my story!

Mickey called her Mother from the pay phone. In the 70s, a public telephone call from a phone booth cost 25 cents. Her family met us at the police station and took her home. I did not think to call home.

I was nervously driving home, still in disbelief, shock, and traumatized over what had just happened. I had not experienced being trauma-informed, so I played the hand I had just been dealt. It was well past when I was supposed to have my Dad's car back, and I did not know what kind of mood he would be in. I explained the situation, and all was forgiven. I don't remember who cleaned Mickey's blood off the back seat of my Dad's Car.

After all that took place, I headed downstate with my High School basketball team and student body to play in the Illinois High School Basketball State Tournament. During the tournament, our basketball team members were called different racial slurs, including ghetto dwellers. Because we were well-coached and understood what was at stake, we steadied our course on the road to the championship. We eventually won after beating three opponents to become the 1973 Chicago Hirsch, Illinois State High School Basketball Champions. After graduating from high school, Mickey and I enjoyed the summer, and I went off to college in the fall.

MY YOUNG ADULT STORY

During my third semester in college, I received a call or letter (I don't remember which one) from Mickey's cousin. She told me that Mickey had been killed in a head-on car collision on a two-lane highway alone with Mickey's cousin. The highway patrol report stated they both were D.O.I., dead on impact. I could not imagine the amount of pain and suffering they endured until taking their last breath.

Mickey's death was my second trauma-related experience with my girlfriend. My latest experience with trauma was a big deal for me because I knew I would not physically have Mickey in my life again. Imagine this: You are 18 years old, away from family and friends, and you receive news that your girl or boyfriend has been killed. I had no grief counselor, no therapist, no spiritual advisor, no nothing to help me cope with this latest tragedy. Memories of Mickey and I getting shot at and Mickey getting shot resurfaced at the forefront of my thoughts. My college classmates knew nothing about what I went through with Mickey. I put it all behind me and out of my mind, so I thought! The news of Mickey's death triggered our past shared trauma experience once again. Now, I was dealing with unresolved past trauma on top of adding another trauma-related experience.

I discussed my unbelievable situation with my college basketball coach, and he was afraid I would not return to school if I went home to Chicago to attend Mickey's homegoing services. He did not want me to leave.

Well, that made me even more mentally upset. I called my parents, and they said all the right things. But I felt alone with my thoughts as to why this happened to Mickey and me after we had just overcome being robbed and shot at. I honestly do not remember if I reached out to my Higher Power during this time. I don't remember saying a prayer.

One of my friends loaned me his car, which had a full tank of gas, and off I went back to Chicago to attend Mickey's funeral. I saw her cousin, Mother, and other family members. After the services, I rested at my parents' house before returning to college. I had already made up my mind that I was going to leave because I felt the coach cared more about my basketball ability than he did about my mental health during my time of need.

Was this a good, bad, right, or wrong decision? I knew I had to make it because my inner guiding system no longer felt comfortable with this coach's lack of remorse, compassion, and leadership, especially when I needed it outside of playing basketball. Remember, I was 18 years old. Making that decision changed my life.

What if my college basketball coach was trauma-informed and understood trauma-related issues? What if he had suggested that I speak with a therapist, psychologist, or spiritual counselor (Pastor/Preacher/Reverend)?

My dear readers, if you need help finding your moment of clarity, three certified addiction recovery coaches share their stories within the pages of this book. Let us assist you as you harness the power of purpose and discover your power within by becoming trauma-informed. We can give you the help I did not receive during my childhood and adolescent years of trauma-related issues.

After leaving college, I felt empty and lost and had no real plan. I began drinking and smoking marijuana like Cheech & Chong in the movie, 'Up In Smoke". I started hanging out in toxic places and doing harmful things with toxic people. None of that mattered at that time. As I look back, I was trying to cope with my post-trauma-related experiences with Mickey, and the solution was alcohol and drugs. From there, I started using cocaine.

I started playing basketball in the summer, trying to return to normal. However, thoughts of losing Mickey to a car accident were ever present all the time. I began having mental obsessions about not being able to be with Mickey, in the flesh, in my arms. She was no longer physically present to cheer me on at my basketball games. The more I became mentally obsessed over the death of Mickey, the more I began to spiral deeper and deeper into alcohol and drugs.

I had a spiritual awakening one morning, and I stopped drinking and drugging and cleaned myself up without any outside intervention. No A.A., Alcoholics Anonymous; at that point in my life, I had not heard of Alcoholics Anonymous, Detox Treatment Centers, The 12-Step Program, a Sponsor, or Halfway Houses. I knew my awakening had to be spiritual because the earthly, human side of me was ready, willing, and able to get as high as a kite and land on cloud nine. But I stopped!

I transferred to another college, played basketball, and got back in order.

<u>MY ADULT STORY</u>

After college, I returned to the same toxic people and places and started doing the same toxic things (alcohol, marijuana, and cocaine). I knew where to score drugs, and it was as easy as buying a gallon of milk. I tried my hand at drug dealing, and I did not like the fact that the cell phone rang every two or three minutes, every day, all day long! The sad and unforgettable part about my short-lived drug dealing days was that both men and women (without thinking a second thought) would do whatever in exchange for drugs. I never asked for sexual favors because of the element of risk that I was not willing to take. I did not misuse or abuse women. I did some dumb things, but I was not stupid!

There were all levels of people, from Main Street to Wall Street, who were scoring drugs—white collar corporate professionals, politicians, doctors, lawyers, law enforcement, firefighters, professional athletes, dentists, husbands, wives, working single mothers, and your everyday man or woman.

I did have a moral compass, and I never, and I do mean never, took advantage of anyone in exchange for drugs. Looking back on those days, I didn't do it for the money. I did it because it looked cool. All the drug dealers were driving nice, flashy cars, had pockets full of money, and drank expensive champagne with top-shelf alcohol on the side. I met many interesting people. I was living the nightlife during my transitional period from working in nightclubs.

During the day, I worked a full-time job. No one at my day job knew about my nightlife, which was fantastic. I was Dr. Jekyll (a well-respected, intelligent person) during the day and Mr. Hyde (the darker side of my existence) at night. In other words, I was living a double life. However, I did accept responsibility for my good, bad, right, and wrong actions.

I had phenomenal cravings during the day, but I never drank or used drugs during working hours. I was always walking on pins and needles because our company had a mandatory random drug testing policy. Once again, my Higher Power watched over me. I did not take a drug test. The level of drugs in my system was enough to register me out of employment. I never considered myself to be an alcoholic or addicted. I know the A.A. 12-step program would say differently. However, I believe that what we confess, we possess – Earl Nightengale. I could accept that I abused alcohol and drugs, but I was not addicted. I did not know what addiction was back then, so I never bought into that terminology.

One morning, after a night of getting high, I came to work, and my eyes were red as a delicious apple. My coworker asked me if there was something wrong with me. I said I was off my square. My coworker thought nothing of it because I never missed a workday. I took an FMLA-Family Medical Leave Act day off, went home, and started getting high. I had a shoebox full of White China cocaine at my disposal. More mental obsessions kicked in, and I was paranoid that if I went back to work and had to take a drug test, I would fail and lose my job. My phenomenal cravings grew stronger and stronger. It got so bad or good that I called in to work and took two weeks of FMLA days off.

During those two weeks, I occasionally got high.

My question for you, my dear readers: Have you ever experienced what seemed to be a miracle during a dark moment in your life?

Well, I woke up one morning and said enough is enough of getting high. My Higher Power came and changed my life forever. I recited my sinner's prayer to my Higher Power. Here are my exact words: Quote: "God, I know I am a sinner. I know I am going to commit other sins. If you take this sin away from me, I will never do this sin again." I went to sleep, and my phenomenal craving for drugs and alcohol no longer existed when I woke up the next day. I put the remaining shoebox half full of cocaine underneath my bed and forgot about it. I went back to work with the 100-pound monkey off my back.

No mental obsessions, no withdrawals, no shaking, no nothing, O.M.G.!

Six months had gone by, and my mind was not on getting high. While looking for one of my shoes underneath my bed, I surprisedly found the shoebox of cocaine. Guess what? My first thought was to start getting high again. My phenomenal craving returned because I was holding a toxic drug (cocaine) in my hands once again. My self-determination was not to spiral back down that destructive path of drinking and drugging, and I made the decision not to drink or use.

My next thought was to go back around the dope houses and sell my half shoebox of cocaine. The street value was worth thousands of dollars. Once again, my self-determination kicked in. I decided against selling drugs because I could not do the time, so I did not do the crime. Finally, I decided to flush the cocaine down the toilet and move on with my life. Why? Remember, I recited my sinner's prayer to my Higher Power. Quote: "God, I know I am a sinner. I know I am going to commit other sins. If you take this sin away from me, I will never do this sin again."

I had enough faith in my sinner's prayer, and more importantly, I wanted to keep my promise of never committing this one sin again. I knocked on the door, and it opened for me. I asked, and it was given unto me. I sought, and I found another way to live. Thanks to my Mother for bringing us into the church environment at a young age. I was very familiar with spirituality, religion, and God, even though I was not an active Sunday go to meeting church attending person during this time in my life. But my faith in my Higher Power was always inside me. My Father showed me how to act like a man. My Mother taught me how and why women deserved respect. During this period in my life, I kept my discretions from them.

I was very intentional with what I needed my Higher Power to do. Now, here's the kicker: I never got drug tested at work, I never lost a job, I never got arrested for possession of illegal substances, I never entered into a detox alcohol and drug rehabilitation treatment center, I never stayed in a halfway house, I never followed the A.A., 12-step program, I never attended any meetings, and I never had a sponsor. I was fully functional, maintaining the highest level of workplace performance because I did understand that the consequences of my action (of discovery) could cost me everything in the blink of an eye. I did see my life flash before me, and what I saw was rock bottom if I did not change my pattern of living. To this day, I have not used any illegal drugs since that faithful day I recited my sinner's prayer to my Higher Power over 40+ years ago.

I met my wife (a Vice President of a Fortune 500 Financial Institution), and we put together a plan of action for success. We are International Speakers, Cofounders of The Mathews Entrepreneur Group, Award-Winning Published Authors (Robbie & Michael), Financial Education Coaches, Streaming Television Show Hosts on JD3TV, Investor Partners in Soothing Salve, and Manuscript Development Specialists/Coaches.

Today, I am a Trauma & Recovery Practitioner and a Certified Addiction Recovery Coach (see my About the Author section for other achievements). I am now better equipped to offer a way out of addiction because of my personal experience.

Coach Michael Bart Mathews – We can use Fifty-Two Shades of Inspiration for one year because It's Time To Get Serious: Finding Your Moment of Clarity Awaits You as You Harness The Power of Purpose.

Fifty-Two Shades of Inspiration: Powered By Your Thoughts, go directly to Amazon: https://a.co/d/81ZS55h.

ABOUT THE AUTHOR

Michael Bart Mathews

Michael "Bart" Mathews is a successful Entrepreneur, Investor, Published Author, Financial Education Coach, Celebrity Interviewer, and International Speaker. Michael and Robbie have been on the same stage as international figureheads worldwide. Such notables as Al Pacino- "The Godfather," John Travolta, 50 Cent-Rapper/Actor, Mark Walberg/Christie Brinkley-Sports Illustrated Cover Girl Super Model/Business Mogul, Bethany Frankel-Founder of Skinny Girl Wine/Calvin Klein-Fashion Designer/Fredrik Eklund-Bravo Television Million Dollar Listing New York/Randi Zuckerberg-former Director of Market Development at Facebook/Mike Ditka 1985 Chicago Bears N.F.L. Super Bowl Champions/ Nelson Mandela's grandson; Nadba Mandela/Kofi Annan-Former Secretary General & joint Noble Peace Prize winner (2001) with the United Nations/Dr. Ervin Laszlo, twice nominated for the Noble Peace Prize in 2004-05/Mirela Sula-Global Woman Magazine Founder/Les Brown, Sir Dr. James Dentley (Presidential Lifetime Achievement Award Recipient) and Lady Dr. Kara Dentley/Jack Canfield, Mark Victor Hanson/Matthew McCaughey/Demi Moore/Wesley Snipes, and Ashton Kutcher; to name a few.

In February 2017, Michael and Robbie shared their International Presentation in the beautiful country of South Africa. Together, they spoke to around 1,200 attendees from 21 countries. Randi Zuckerberg and Nelson Mandela's grandson, Ndaba Mandela, were also speaking. Robbie interviewed Ndaba Mandela on that stage after Michael and Robbie delivered a powerful presentation.

On May 10, 2017, Michael and Robbie attended retired N.F.L. player Marques Odgen's Speaker Academy with other N.F.L. players, Walt Harris, Justin C. Smith, Kyle Bradey, Donte Jones, and other business professionals.

On July 15, 2017, Michael and Robbie shared the stage with more talented people. High-profile personalities like Suzanne Le` Mignot-CBS Channel 2 News Journalist, D. Channsin Berry-Film Producer, and Cynda Williams-Actress (Spike Lee) were there. Others included Tony Grant-Singer/Actor (Tyler Perry) and event organizer Quinton de` Alexander at the "We Dream In Color Humanitarian Celebration." In addition, Michael received the Businessman of the Year award, named after John H. Johnson, founder of Ebony & Jet Magazine, in honor of his humanitarian efforts to help make this world better.

Michael is the co-founder of The Mathews Entrepreneur Group (TMEG). He is dedicated to providing Personal Development and Financial Literacy education programs and one-on-one financial literacy guidance using books, workshops, online programs, and one-on-one personal results coaching. Michael will also provide entertaining and exciting books for pleasure reading. Property investors and land banking can also be added to their generational wealth-building portfolio.

He is also the founder of WeCreateBooks. Mission Statement: We empower you to tell your story and get your book out of your head so it can be published and read. Michael has personally authored Financially Speaking, Finding Your Moment of Clarity, and Fifty-Two Shades of Inspiration and co-authored additional books. He has personally coached more than 200 writers from 15 countries, with 90 becoming published authors, 13 achieving number two best-sellers, and one new book release.

Michael was born and raised on the south side of Chicago, Illinois. As a young adult, he attended Bray Temple C.M.E. Church, where his spiritual guidance was nurtured. He was educated in the Chicago Public School System, graduating from Paul Revere Elementary School and Hirsch High School.

While attending Hirsch High School, Michael was a 1973 Boys Class AA Chicago City Basketball Championship team member and the (IHSA) Class A.A. Illinois State High School Basketball Championship Team member. The State Championship team was inducted into the Illinois High School Association (IHSA) Hall of Fame Class of 1993 and the Chicago Public League Basketball Coaches Association (CPLBCA) Hall of Fame Class of 2013. Michael was also inducted into Chicago Hirsch High School's Alumni Hall of Fame Class of 2016.

Michael did his undergraduate studies at Lincoln University in Jefferson City, Missouri, and the University of Wisconsin-Parkside in Kenosha, Wisconsin, where he played basketball at both universities.

Michael spent 30 years in the private and public transportation sectors, holding trainer/management positions in the private sector and operator/line instructor positions in the public sector, before retiring from the Chicago Transit Authority in 2012.

Michael's call to service stems from his burning desire and heartfelt mission to give back to society. During his employment with the Chicago Transit Authority, he regularly donated to the Historically Black Colleges and Universities Scholarship Fund to help grow our future leaders.

<u>They are board members of the Always Already Amazing Charitable Foundation, started by their dear friends, Sir Dr. James and Dame Dr. Kara Dentley, in the Chicagoland Area. Together, we assist, inspire, change, and transform the lives of children, seniors, and Veterans using various programs. They are also Benefactors of the Monarchical Chapter of the Sovereign And Royal House of Cappadocia.</u>

Michael and Robbie Mathews have been internationally featured in the media: Saturday Star and the Sunday Times News Papers, Kaya FM and 93.8FM radio, and ANN7 Television in South Africa. While on the French Rivera in Cannes, France, they were featured on the airwaves of Radio France. They were also mentioned on the front cover of the Las Vegas Hollywood (L.V.H.) Dubain magazine, and in a seven-page pictorial and print article.

In addition, Robbie has graced the cover of the Global Woman Magazine; Michael has been featured on the cover of the Global Man Magazine based in London and WORKLIFE Magazine in Australia, and Business Booster Today in Germany. They have been featured on local radio in the Chicagoland area on 102.3FM, Always Amazing T.V. & CAN-TV (Chicago Access Network Television), Punch T.V. in Los Angeles, and JD3TV in Orland Park, Illinois.

Michael and his wife, Robbie, are investor partners in Soothing Salve. They reside in Illinois and enjoy serving others, continuing education, International Speaking, writing, traveling, and spending time with their grandchildren. They are lifelong learners enrolled in the University of Lifeology.

Visit his website at www.tmeginc.com

https://Linktr.ee/michaelbartmathews
https://tmeginc.com/testimonials
https://www.facebook.com/michaelbartmathews
https://www.linkedin.com/in/michaelbartmathews
https://www.instagram.com/michaelbartmathews
Business: 1/708/634/6785
Email: wecreatebooks@tmeginc.com

CHAPTER THREE
FACED DEFEAT BUT NEVER DEFEATED
KGABO LUCIA MANTHATA
(SOUTH AFRICA)

"Legacy is not leaving material things but leaving yourself in everyone's heart. This is what l strive for every day of my life." – *Kgabo Lucia Manthata.*

The difference between you and me is very minimal. l have been broke, hungry, exploited, mocked, hurt, and demotivated, leading to low self-esteem, just like many others. What changed my life was believing that failure is not an option.

"Faced Defeat But Never Defeated" is a chapter that I authored with the intention of offering support and motivation to women who have navigated through immense challenges such as abuse, divorce, rejection, and the loss of their identity and self-worth. My chapter is aimed at those who have found themselves single parents, faced the difficulties of divorce, or endured abuse in any form.

This book conveys empowerment, resilience, and encouragement for women to believe in their inherent strength and potential. Despite women's adversities, it emphasizes that they can achieve greatness and deserve to dream and embark on a new chapter in life, regardless of their past struggles. It serves as a beacon of hope, reminding them that it is never too late to begin anew and reclaim their self-worth and purpose.

"Faced Defeat But Never Defeated" stands out from other personal development self-help books aimed at women facing similar challenges through its unique blend of personal narrative, practical advice, and empowering guidance. Here are some key differentiators:

PERSONAL TOUCH:

This chapter draws upon the author's (own) experiences, making it profoundly relatable and authentic. Sharing my (personal) stories of overcoming adversity establishes a strong connection with readers who may see themselves reflected in the narrative.

PRACTICAL STRATEGIES:

In addition to inspirational content, my chapter offers concrete strategies and actionable steps that women can implement in their lives. I provide tools for self-reflection, goal setting, and resilience-building, enabling readers to work towards positive change.

EMPOWERMENT FOCUS:

Rather than just offering sympathy or commiseration, *"Faced Defeat But Never Defeated"* seeks to empower women to take control of their (own) narratives and futures. It emphasizes inner strength, self-belief, and each individual's limitless potential.

MESSAGE OF RESILIENCE:

Central to the book is the message that while defeat may be a temporary setback, defeat only occurs when one gives up. It instills a sense of resilience and perseverance, encouraging women to keep moving forward in the face of adversity.

Combining these elements, *"Faced Defeat But Never Defeated"* provides a unique, impactful resource for women seeking to overcome hardships and cultivate renewed empowerment and purpose.

OVERCOMING CHILDHOOD ADVERSITY:

As a child of parents who divorced, I know all too well the impact divorce can have on a young mind. The feelings of worthlessness, shame, and confusion that consumed me after my parents' separation were overwhelming. I felt like my voice didn't matter - like my pain was insignificant during the chaos around me. I blamed myself for my parents' divorce. I remember my mom leaving us alone with my sister so that she could drink alcohol. My dad would beat her, and I felt that maybe if I were not born, they would have stayed together, as most of the fights were about her not doing her motherly duties due to her drinking. This internalized guilt led to a deep sense of inadequacy and low self-esteem that followed me into adulthood. It took years of healing and self-reflection to realize that their divorce was not my fault and that I was worthy of love and success just like anyone else.

I wish there had been more support available to help me navigate the emotional turmoil of my parents' divorce. Counseling and therapy could have provided me with the tools and resources to cope with my feelings and move forward in a healthy way. Instead, I struggled and suffered in silence, feeling isolated and misunderstood.

But now, looking back, I see that my pain has made me stronger. I have used my experiences as motivation to succeed and prove to myself and others that I am more than just a product of divorce. I believe that every "child of divorce" has the potential to overcome their past and find fulfillment in life, but only if they are given the support and validation they need to heal.

When I reflect on my childhood experiences with my parent's divorce and being raised by a stepmother and a father, I have positive experiences. I can't help but also acknowledge the negative impact it had on me. I was constantly criticized and painted as a "bad child" all the time. The criticism lowered my self-esteem, trust in others, and ability to form healthy relationships. These challenges followed me into adulthood, affecting my personal life and overall well-being. Seeking therapy helped me navigate through these struggles and work towards personal growth. This is a reminder of the importance of addressing past traumas and seeking support to heal and move forward.

ROOTED IN RESILIENCE: A JOURNEY OF FAITH AND FORTITUDE

From my upbringing in a household steeped in Christian values, I have been anchored in the unwavering foundation of faith. I accepted Jesus Christ as my Savior at the age of ten. This steadfast connection to Christ has been a beacon of strength, illuminating the path forward even in the darkest times. As a child, I instinctively embraced challenges with a spirit of resilience that belied my tender years. This innate quality, nurtured by the teachings of my faith, shaped my worldview and instilled in me a steadfast resolve to confront adversity head-on. Each trial became an opportunity for growth, and each setback was a lesson in perseverance.

However, despite my unwavering faith and inner strength, the core of my resilience was put to the ultimate test in the realm of marriage. This sacred union, once a source of joy and companionship, gradually evolved into a crucible of trials and tribulations that shook the very foundations of my being.

Through the lens of my personal experiences, I aim to offer a raw and unfiltered account of the struggles within my marriage, shedding light on the complexities of relationships and the profound impact they can have on one's sense of self. I sincerely hope that by sharing my story, others grappling with similar challenges may find solace, inspiration, and hope amidst the storm.

In marriages and relationships, individuals often encounter various challenges when dealing with specific behaviors of their spouses. These are my personal experiences.

Feeling Threatened: A partner exhibited controlling and manipulative behaviors, causing a lack of trust and emotional distress. He would force me to allow him to attend my business meetings. He would do clandestine searches on people I interacted with and accuse me of inappropriate relationships with male business associates.

DECEPTION ABOUT SEXUALITY:

A partner was dishonest about his sexuality or sexual preference, leading to feelings of betrayal and confusion. Arguments arose over his close male friend, whom he fiercely defended even when I was full of suspicion. There was a situation where he was hurt by this "friend," and I somehow had to support him emotionally.

The shadows of physical and emotional abuse loomed large over my life, casting a dark veil that engulfed me in fear and isolation. The physical abuse I endured in my marriage also left me battered and broken, with wounds that ran deep not just on the surface but within my very soul. The pain of being beaten was not just skin-deep; it seared through me, leaving behind scars that may never fully heal. It led me down a path riddled with fear and uncertainty, which seemed to have no end. As the bruises faded, the emotional scars remained festering beneath the surface like an open wound. The emotional abuse inflicted upon me made me question my worth, leaving me feeling worthless and insignificant. Anxiety and depression became constant companions, their grip tightening with each passing day.

In the darkest hour of my life, I found myself teetering on the brink of despair. The trauma I endured pushed me to the edge, and on that fateful night, I almost succumbed to the overwhelming darkness by taking my own life. Directly (same day at night) after my suicide attempt, when we got home, my then-husband, in a twisted act of cruelty, violated me sexually against my will, claiming it was a twisted form of "makeup sex." Even after I fought and cried trying to stop him, the pain of that betrayal cut deep, leaving me shattered and lost. I was confused because I did not legally see (then) how my husband could rape me.

Seeking solace and understanding after my divorce, I turned to a psychologist for help. Through our sessions, I uncovered the layers of trauma that had built up within me. The psychologist's gentle guidance helped me realize that the reactions and behaviors I exhibited were akin to those of individuals who had suffered sexual violations. It was then that the floodgates of suppressed memories opened, and I found myself reliving a painful past.

Embracing the truth of my experiences, I confronted the buried memories of sexual violations that I had long suppressed. The tears that flowed washed away the veil of denial, revealing a reality I could no longer ignore. It was a journey of healing and self-discovery, fraught with challenges but illuminated by the flickering flame of hope.

<u>UNDERMINING DREAMS:</u>

My then-husband belittled my aspirations, resulting in frustration, resentment, and unfulfillment.

FINANCIAL CONTROL:

He manipulated finances, leaving me financially dependent and unable to leave the toxic relationship due to a lack of resources. This financial abuse is a common barrier for many women in similar situations.

GASLIGHTING:

Through manipulation, my ex-husband distorted reality, making me doubt my (own) perceptions and experiences.

VERBAL ABUSE:

Enduring verbal abuse took a toll on my emotional well-being, causing pain, low self-esteem, and a sense of powerlessness.

DEALING WITH A NARCISSIST:

A narcissistic spouse can be emotionally draining, as their self-centered behavior can lead to manipulation and exploitation of their partner for personal gain. This often results in severe mental health consequences for the affected. I know a few people who ended up in a mental health hospital due to this.

Being married to a narcissistic spouse can feel like a never-ending battle. I remember constantly feeling like I was walking on eggshells, trying to please someone who was never satisfied. The emotional toll it took on me was immense, and I often felt lost and helpless.

As the divorce process began, things only escalated. My ex-spouse became increasingly manipulative, using every tactic possible to try to manipulate the process. It became a constant struggle to protect myself and my rights, but I knew I had to stand up for myself and fight for what was fair.

I sought help wherever I could find it. My friends and family provided a strong support system, helping me through the darkest days. Throughout it all, I made sure to prioritize self-care. I set boundaries with my ex-spouse, refusing to engage in his toxic behavior. I focused on my (own) well-being, taking time to heal and rebuild myself after the damage had been done.

If you find yourself in a similar situation, know there is hope. You are not alone, and there are people who can help you through this difficult time. Remember to prioritize yourself, seek support from those around you, and empower yourself to fight for what you deserve. You are stronger than you think and will come out of this stronger and more resilient than ever.

During this challenging period, he violated the court order regarding child custody, taking our daughter as he pleased and deciding when he would bring her back without consulting with me. On one occasion, he involved the police, falsely accusing me of stealing a car. He came with the cops and confiscated the vehicle in a public space. This incident caused immense embarrassment, and I had to rely on public transport for my children and me.

Having no vehicle made the situation more difficult because my son was involved in sports activities, requiring transportation to various games. Regular taxis did not service our destination, forcing us to use metered taxis, which were extremely expensive. Despite these challenges, I persevered, determined to overcome the obstacles thrown my way.

During my bouts of abuse, I found myself engaging in a way I never imagined I would in an effort to cope with the pain and protect my children. I used makeup to hide physical scars (I had never liked makeup before the abuse started). I also compromised my values in hopes of change that never came. Loyalty and love drove me to lie on behalf of my abuser husband, to paint his false image of perfection to conceal the brokenness within. Only later did I realize that these lies would be used against me, manipulating my words to further his advantage. The cycle of abuse led to compromising my interests and desires, shifting my focus to try and please the abuser instead of honoring my own needs. But despite my efforts to impress and please, the abuser remained indifferent, failing to appreciate my sacrifices.

It is a harrowing experience to live a life of deception and self-sacrifice and navigate the complexities of abuse. The facade of a picture-perfect family masking the turmoil and pain within serves as a stark reminder of the toll abuse takes on one's sense of self and identity.

It is crucial for anyone experiencing these difficulties in marriage to seek support and help from trusted individuals or organizations. Your safety and well-being should always be a top priority.

As a Christian woman, I understood it's important to lean on my faith during this difficult time.

HERE ARE SOME STEPS I TOOK TO REBUILD MY LIFE AFTER DIVORCE:

1. Turned to prayer and sought guidance from God for strength, wisdom, and healing.
2. Surrounded myself with a supportive community of friends, family, and church members for love and encouragement.
3. Sought counseling or therapy to work through emotional challenges and gain perspective on moving forward.
4. Took care of myself physically, emotionally, and spiritually through self-care activities.
5. Joined a support group for divorced individuals to connect with others going through similar experiences.
6. Focused on personal growth and rediscovered my passions and interests.
7. Worked towards forgiveness for myself and my ex-spouse, finding closure and peace.
8. Stayed connected to my faith through worship, prayer, and scripture, trusting in God's plan for my life even in this season of change.

FINDING HEALING AFTER DIVORCE:

After my divorce, I realized that healing and forgiveness were essential for moving forward in a positive way. I allowed myself to grieve at the end of my marriage and focused on taking care of myself physically, emotionally, and spiritually. I contacted friends, family, and a counselor for support and talked about my feelings and experiences, which helped me gain perspective.

I practiced forgiveness towards myself and my ex-spouse, knowing that it was a process that required time and patience. Engaging in activities like journaling, therapy, and joining a support group for divorced individuals helped me promote healing and growth. I focused on rebuilding my life, exploring new hobbies and interests, and finding new purpose and fulfillment.

Staying connected to my faith and trusting in a Higher Power gave me guidance and strength throughout the healing and forgiveness process. It's important to remember that healing and forgiveness are ongoing journeys that require patience and self-compassion. By allowing myself to grieve, seek support, practice forgiveness, and focus on personal growth.

Therapy alone didn't provide the relief needed. It wasn't until I went to a Bible College that I finally found total healing, forgiveness, and peace. The word of God became my source of comfort, guiding me towards a path that therapy couldn't. The assignments at college required me to confront truths and deal with them head-on. Some of the tasks were so emotionally challenging that I found myself writing while crying, as they brought back all the emotions of anger, hatred, and pain. But through these problematic assignments, I was able to work through past traumas that I thought I dealt with and come out stronger on the other side."

Dealing with abuse and overcoming it can be a challenging process, but it's essential to prioritize your safety and well-being.

HERE ARE SOME STEPS YOU CAN TAKE:

1. Seek support: Reach out to trusted friends, family members, or support organizations for help and guidance. You don't have to go through this alone.
2. Create a safety plan: Develop a plan to keep yourself safe if abuse escalates. This may include identifying safe places to go, keeping important documents and emergency contacts handy, and setting boundaries with the abuser.
3. Consider therapy: Counseling or therapy can help you process your experiences, heal from the trauma, and develop coping strategies for dealing with the abuse.

4. Educate yourself: Learn more about the different forms of abuse, understand your rights, and explore available resources.

5. Set boundaries: Assert your boundaries with the abuser and (clearly) communicate your needs. It's important to prioritize your well-being and safety.

6. Consider seeking legal help: If the abuse is severe or ongoing, consider seeking legal assistance to protect yourself and take necessary legal action.

Remember, it's never your fault, and you deserve to be treated with respect and dignity. You have the strength to overcome abuse and build a healthier, happier life.

After enduring various forms of abuse, I have managed to achieve incredible success in my entrepreneurial journey. From winning prestigious awards to being a finalist in pageants, I have proven that hard work, self-determination, and a passion for empowering others can lead to great accomplishments. My involvement in mentorship programs and business competitions showcases my commitment to giving back to the community and helping aspiring entrepreneurs reach their full potential.

As a board member at a tertiary hospital and a luxury lifestyle estate, I dedicated myself to making a positive impact in the business world and the community. By living by the motto, "Living a legacy is not about leaving material things but about leaving a piece of yourself in each endeavor," I strive to exemplify the true spirit of entrepreneurship – using my skills and resources to create a lasting impact on the world around me.

NEW RELATIONSHIPS:

Navigating the complexities of a blended family after divorce can be challenging, especially in today's world, where such family dynamics are increasingly common. One significant hurdle individuals face when entering a new relationship is dealing with the dynamics of co-parenting with their ex-partners.

The situation can become even more complicated when jealousy arises from one towards the ex-partner moving on and attempting to disrupt the new relationship, often by involving the children. This jealousy can lead to a power struggle, particularly when multiple parents—up to four to six, depending on the number of kids and parents involved—have different opinions on raising the children in the shared household. This includes reconciling various beliefs, morals, and values within the blended family setting.

Ultimately, what may begin as a harmonious relationship between a couple can be significantly impacted by conflicts stemming from the actions of the ex-partners. Finding a way to navigate these challenges and establish a united front in co-parenting can be essential for the success and stability of the new blended family.

<u>**HERE ARE SOME CHALLENGES YOU MAY FACE:**</u>

1. Differences in parenting styles: Each parent may have their own approach to disciplining and raising children, leading to conflicts when blending two families together.
2. Resentment and jealousy: The ex-partner who has not moved on may feel resentful or jealous of the new relationship and family dynamics, leading to tension and conflict within the blended family.
3. Children's adjustment: Children may struggle to adapt to the new family structure, particularly if they feel caught in the middle of their parents' emotions and conflicts.
4. Communication barriers: Effective communication is critical in any relationship, but it can be incredibly challenging in blended families with multiple parents and children involved.
5. Co-parenting arrangements: Coordinating schedules, making decisions together, and maintaining consistency in parenting can be difficult when dealing with blended family dynamics.

Couples in blended families must prioritize open communication, empathy, and patience to navigate these challenges successfully. Seeking support from a therapist or counselor can also be beneficial in helping to address any underlying issues and work towards a harmonious family environment.

All members must prioritize communication, understanding, and empathy to mitigate these challenges in blended families.

<u>**HERE ARE SOME STRATEGIES THAT CAN HELP**</u>

1. Establish clear boundaries and expectations within the family unit.

2. Encourage open and honest communication between all family members.
3. Create a sense of unity and teamwork within the family, emphasizing the importance of working together towards common goals.
4. Respect each other's differences and parenting styles, find ways to compromise, and find common ground.

5. Seek support from a therapist or counselor to address any underlying issues and learn healthy coping strategies.
6. Take time to bond and create positive experiences as a family.
7. Practice patience and understanding, recognizing that blending families takes time and effort.

By implementing these strategies and prioritizing the well-being of all family members, blended families can successfully navigate the challenges they face and build a strong, cohesive family unit.

Blended families, consisting of stepparents, stepchildren, and half-siblings, face unique challenges that can impact the dynamics and relationships within the family unit. One of the primary challenges blended families face is navigating the complex emotions and loyalty conflicts that arise from combining two separate families into one cohesive unit.

Children may struggle with feelings of loyalty to their biological parent and resentment towards their stepparent, leading to tension and discord within the family. Additionally, stepchildren may feel like outsiders in the new family structure, resulting in isolation and rejection.

Another challenge blended families face is establishing new roles and boundaries. Stepparents may struggle to find their place in the family hierarchy, while biological parents may find it challenging to delegate authority and decision-making to their spouse. This can lead to power struggles and conflicts as each family member adjusts to their new roles and responsibilities.

Communication is also a key challenge for blended families, as each member may have different communication styles and expectations. Effective communication is essential for resolving conflicts, addressing issues, and building solid relationships within the family. Without open and honest communication, misunderstandings and misinterpretations can lead to further tension and division.

Therefore, the people who suffer the most from all this are 'THE CHILDREN.' It's time for society to recognize the struggles of children of divorce, listen to their stories, and acknowledge their pain. By providing the necessary resources and support, we can empower these children to break free from the cycle of insecurity and self-doubt. We can ensure their voices are heard and valued and they are given the opportunity to thrive and succeed despite their past.

In conclusion, domestic abuse is a pervasive issue that affects individuals from all walks of life. It is crucial for victims to seek help and support in order to break free from the cycle of abuse. Through my experience, I have learned the power of forgiveness and the importance of prioritizing my well-being. I hope my story can serve as a beacon of hope for others facing similar challenges and remind them that they deserve love, respect, and dignity.

As I reflect on those difficult times, I am reminded of the strength and resilience that allowed me to endure such immense suffering. In these moments of darkness, I turned to God and found solace in the power of forgiveness. Despite the betrayal and cruelty I faced, I made the courageous choice to forgive my ex-partners, not for his sake, but for my (own) well-being.

Forgiveness was not an easy path to tread. It required me to confront my pain head-on and release the anger and resentment that threatened to consume me. Through the act of forgiveness, I was able to free myself from the chains of bitterness and find a sense of peace within my soul. In forgiving my ex-partners, I reclaimed my power and emerged from the shadows of despair with a renewed sense of purpose.

Today, as I stand tall in the light of healing and forgiveness, I am filled with gratitude for the journey that brought me to this place of wholeness. I have learned that I deserve love, respect, and dignity. My past does not define me. I am not just a survivor. I am a thriver, a warrior who has weathered the storms of life and emerged stronger on the other side.

To anyone experiencing similar struggles, I urge you to seek help and support and never lose faith in your worth and potential. You are not alone, and you are worthy of a life filled with joy and fulfillment. Forgiveness is not a sign of weakness but a courageous act of self-love and healing. Embrace forgiveness and watch it transform your life in ways you never thought possible.

In reflecting on the tumultuous chapters of my past, I am reminded of the profound resilience that resides within the depths of the human spirit. As I recount the harrowing experiences endured in the wake of abusive relationships with both of my former husbands, a stark reality emerges—one defined by the enduring impact of trauma and the transformative power of personal growth.

Having experienced the tumultuous terrain of matrimony twice over, the weight of societal judgment looms heavily upon my shoulders. The mere mention of my two divorces often elicits disdainful glances and whispered conjectures, casting a shadow of doubt upon my character. Yet, what remains unseen are the clandestine scars etched upon my soul, the silent narratives of suffering and survival that have sculpted the contours of my being.

The insidious nature of abuse, both physical and emotional, left an indelible mark on my spirit, shattering the illusion of marital bliss and exposing the raw vulnerabilities that lay dormant within. The echoes of manipulation and cruelty still reverberate, serving as a poignant reminder of the tumultuous terrain I once navigated with trembling resolve.

In the wake of such harrowing tribulations, I stand before the world not as a victim of circumstance but as a testament to the unwavering strength that resides within the human heart. The judgments cast by society pale in comparison to the fortitude cultivated through adversity. A resilience born of the crucible of pain and tempered by the fires of transformation are now present.

As I confront the lingering stigma attached to the label of "divorcee," I am reminded of the power inherent in reclaiming one's narrative, of seizing control of the pen and inscribing a new chapter of empowerment and self-discovery. It is not the number of times one has loved and lost that defines one's worth, but rather the courage exhibited in the pursuit of healing and wholeness.

So, to those who would dare to question the intricacies of my story, I say this—the shadows of my past do not define me. I am encouraged by the light that shines forth from within. My journey is an experience woven with threads of resilience and redemption, a testament to the enduring power of the human spirit to rise, phoenix-like, from the ashes of despair.

In the heart of my suffering, I discovered the wellspring of strength that lies dormant within us all, a font of resilience from which I draw sustenance in the face of adversity. And though the road ahead may be fraught with unknown challenges, I walk forward with my head held high, secure in the knowledge that I am a thriver, a warrior, a beacon of hope for those who may yet find themselves adrift in the tumultuous seas of life.

This is my truth, my testament to the enduring power of the human spirit in the face of adversity. In sharing my story, I dare to hope others may find solace, inspiration, and the courage to embrace their journey with unwavering grace and unyielding strength.

ABOUT THE AUTHOR

Kgabo Lucia Manthata

After overcoming significant hardships, I have emerged as one of the most inspirational and innovative women in South Africa. My achievements include winning prestigious awards like:

- The Engine Pitch
- Polish Pitch Perfect Competitions
- The Standard Bank Top Woman Award

I was recognized as one of South Africa's top 50 female business founders and have successfully established three preschools, "Little Harvey's Kids Academy," across different provinces in Secunda, Whiteriver, and Thohoyandou (South Africa).

Through media features and interviews, I have shared my journey and insights, culminating in the publication of "The Confident Entrepreneur," Available on Amazon.

Paperback link: https://amzn.to/3vAZ35y
Ebook link: https://amzn.to/3vEMQx1

The Confident Entrepreneur is a comprehensive guide for aspiring business owners. My story is a testament to the power of resilience and determination, inspiring others to pursue their dreams with unwavering belief in themselves.

Kgabo Lucia Manthata

Motivational Speaker|Entrepreneur|Business and Life Coach:
For bookings: klmanthata@gmail.com
+27769934517(call and WhatsApp)

IF I CAN DO IT, SO CAN YOU!

CHAPTER FOUR
MY ADVERSITIES BECAME
MY SEEDS OF GREATNESS
SHERRI PICKET (USA)

I am the go-to person. It's been this way my entire life. Everyone has always had trust and interest in my thoughts, decisions, and opinions. For the most part, I have always been confident in my decisions regarding responsibilities and business, but matters of the heart were different. Sure, I give great insight and revelation on another person's relationship, but when it came to how I handled myself, let's say loving you is a process. My story begins here.

I was silly enough to marry at 22 years old, and at the time, I thought it was the absolute "right" thing to do. I was in love with a hot head who wouldn't allow anyone to bother a hair on my head, except for him, of course. Yes, some things were intriguing about him. He wasn't highly educated, didn't make much money, wasn't the nicest person, nor did he know how to compliment my swag. But what he did have made me overlook all the qualities he lacked. At the end of the day, I ate whatever he was serving.

Sure, there were signs before we married, but who pays attention? You know how we do: We keep making up lies and excuses for why we tolerate the constant disrespect and abuse until we believe them. Then, one day, your point of view changes, but not before the distractions.

On Friday nights, we hosted parties at a bar in downtown Detroit with a group of our friends. We always had a great time hanging out with our friends, dancing, and socializing with guests who came to the party. My husband, at the time, had two main weaknesses that never mixed with anything, alcohol, and women. He was a true ladies' man; he loved everything about women and knew how to please them. You see, for a woman who hasn't learned how to control or operate with a partner who gives good sex, this is the thing that can change how she feels about everything. I'll tell you the way I have thought about my daughter, DICK MAKES YOU DUMB! I was completely dumb concerning the things this man did. Now, back to the story.

As usual, I'm on the dance floor, moving and shaking. I love to dance! I never cared much about drinking and smoking, but dancing is my thing. As I engaged in the music and the other girls laughing on the dance floor alongside me, my husband was all over this beautiful young lady. He always thought I wasn't hip to all his behind-my-head ways with women. I could tell from a distance that he was trying his best to get her number. She smiled and rubbed his face, and that sealed it for me. I didn't make any scenes, and I NEVER did. I always played it cool like nothing he ever did was a big deal, at least in front of people.

As we wrapped up the night, said goodbye to our friends, and headed to the car, I told him I had seen his interaction with the beautiful girl. He immediately got defensive and belligerent. He started cursing and yelling as he was driving us home. We were speeding on the Lodge Freeway, arguing about the inappropriate interaction that I had (clearly) witnessed.

Out of his frustration of trying to browbeat me into believing that I didn't see what I (clearly) saw and to make it seem like his action with her was purely business. He tried to hit me but missed because it's hard to hit someone and drive. Well, he does the next best thing.

As we exit the freeway and cut through the neighborhood to get to Vassar St, which would take us the rest of the way home, he hits the gas to increase his speed and crashes the car into a tree! I didn't have my seatbelt on; it was God's grace because the airbags deployed, and I didn't go through the windshield. He put the car in reverse and drove us the rest of the way home, with the car leaking several fluids. My chest was hurting from the impact of the airbag. Tears were streaming down my face. I knew then he could kill me.

This wasn't the first time he showed anger towards me, nor the first time he had been abusive to me. However, it was the first time I realized how serious my situation was. He could not control his emotions, nor did he have the ability to control his actions, and this could lead me to death. I don't want any man who has the mentality that he loves me so much that he would kill me because he can't live without me.

After that day, I was planning my escape. I didn't know how everything would fall in line, but I knew it was time to go. My male best friend, at the time, was willing to help with whatever I needed, but he also complicated things for me and his relationship. My friend and I loved one another and believed we had since middle school, but now was not the time for me to get wrapped in a man, no matter who he was.

I was messed up mentally and emotionally, and I needed a friend, not another lover. This wasn't my friend's fault; this was the nature of our relationship. Over the years, no matter who we dated or were with, we always found our way back to one another, and yes, it would always become physical. Since I had been with my husband, my friend did not interact this way. We talked as friends, but the sexual part of our relationship was put on hold. That is until my husband became abusive, and my marriage was falling apart. I remember the day I said, "the hell with this, I'm going to play his game." I will let no man make a fucking fool out of me.

I was a flight attendant for a smaller airline and sold real estate; I was a hustler. I was returning from a three-day trip and couldn't wait to get home. Believe it or not, I always missed my then-husband when I was away from him. I truly loved this man. I saw so much potential in him, and he/we could have done great things together.

I am riding home singing and rapping (I also love to rap), feeling good, and can't wait to get home. As I approach the house, I see his car sitting in the driveway, and I'm like, yes, he's home! I get out of the car, eager to get into the house to see my husband. I open the door, and I hear voices and rustling around. Walking through the kitchen into my dining room, I see two individuals: my husband and a woman I had never seen before. With a confused look, I said, "Hey, what's going on?" My husband replies, "Hey, babe, I forgot you were coming home. This is my friend blah blah. I'm doing a photo shoot for her." The woman tried to play it off, but I could tell this was more than a business interaction. I looked at the woman, said hello, and immediately headed upstairs. He was on my heels right behind me. I was calm, and that scared him more than I was irate.

The truth was that his hypnosis of charm, strength, and lovemaking was wearing off. I would've done anything for this man. I compromised so many parts of myself to make him happy that I forgot I was the prize. He was blessed to have me and not the other way around. But I am thinking, if I play everything cool and can be down for whatever, let us do threesomes with other women, and have his back, he would give me everything I need and want. <u>Hell</u> to the <u>No</u>!

He was never a real protector, provider, lover, or trustworthy friend. He cared about only himself. He would say or do anything he had to get his way. He seriously did not care about anyone, not for real. I often watched him disrespect his sisters and mother, so I knew I was no exception. I was dumb to him and his ways, but now I was becoming numb.

As I put my bags down and started to get ready to shower, he came upstairs (still on my heels), trying to plead his case, although he did so with a bit of hostility in his voice. He had the nerve to try and have an attitude, really? I allowed him to ramble for a few minutes, then assured him everything was fine and I wasn't mad. At this point, he could say whatever he wanted. I didn't care to have him lie in my face. There wasn't even a car parked outside, meaning he picked this heifer up, and maybe she was spending the night.

I don't know, but I do know she was going to stay awhile, which was obvious. So, once I got my husband out of my face, he returned downstairs with his female friend. I showered, dressed, and called my homeboy and told him I was on the way to see him. Of course, my homeboy was happy that I was coming. I walked past my husband and his friend and told them I was leaving and have a great night. I will be back sometime later. Oh, I knew this was going to get under my husband's skin, but he wasn't going to show his ass in front of this woman he was trying to impress. So, I took full advantage of this rare opportunity. Remember, I said <u>Hell</u> to the <u>No!</u> I got in my car and left. I did not fully understand that I was only making matters worse, not better.

Since that day, two things happened: I realized my husband didn't truly love me, and he realized I was figuring him out. My husband was going out of his way to be nice to me. He even started to be somewhat romantic. He was making love to me as if he missed me and needed to keep me close to him. I, on the other hand, was doing what I needed to do until I could exit stage left. This meant pretending everything was all good until the day came when I could escape. I knew this would be a bittersweet day for me, but it was a step I needed to take.

On one random weekday, my husband left for work as usual. I cooked dinner the night before, and we got along incredible. We even made love. It was perfect, but not enough to change the course of events the following day.

After my husband turned the corner for work, a small moving truck pulled up from the opposite direction. A few of my girlfriends pulled up just minutes after the moving truck, and in about 2 hours, I moved out of my big, pretty house and on my way to a 2-bedroom apartment. I thought I was ready to start things fresh and move on.

My homeboy wanted me to be madly in love with him, but I couldn't at the time. My husband broke my heart, and I wasn't in the right head space to make these decisions. I had to recover from some trauma-related issues. I needed true healing, and I couldn't heal the way I needed to if I were in another relationship, especially with someone else I truly loved. This was one of the closest men to me, and I didn't want to mess up our relationship by starting something I wasn't ready to finish.

My husband called, texted, and pleaded his case for two weeks. He cried that he missed me and would do better if I just came home, and for the most part, I wasn't buying it. It sounded like the same old excuses, and he would say anything to get his way.

I was standing my ground until I agreed to meet him face to face. I was coming from an overnight flight, so I decided to meet my husband, the man I ran away from, at the Cracker Barrell near the airport. Let me tell you, I didn't know I missed him until I saw him, and it was downhill from there. I returned to our house, and he convinced me we could work it out. Once I returned to my apartment, I had to explain my decision to my homeboy. My homeboy claimed he understood, but his heart was a little broken. Within a week, I moved out of the apartment and back home. I wanted to give my marriage another try. Let's see how this goes.

I can't keep anything down, and the room is spinning. I'm used to dealing with an upset stomach, but this was hurting so bad I had to head to the emergency section at the hospital. It turns out it was a stomach virus that should pass in a few days. I was told to follow up with my doctor in a couple of days after taking the medicine the ER doctor prescribed. A few days passed, and I didn't see much improvement, but I was sitting in my primary care doctor's office, and I knew whatever this was, he would be able to help me get myself together.

Dr. Harrison greeted me with a pleasant smile, as always. "What seems to be the matter, asked Dr. Harrison?" I told him I had a stomach bug, per the hospital, but the medicine didn't work. He nodded, smiled, and said he would have some test run to see what was happening. The nurse took some blood and urine, and after about 10 minutes, Dr. Harrison entered the room. He looked at me intently and asked who my OBGYN was. I replied I didn't have one! Your office did my pap smears. He laughed, then informed me that's all about to change. Confused, I asked why this was going to change things. That's when he said the line that changed my life forever. You're pregnant!

In a state of complete shock, I denied it and said that the hospital stated it was a stomach virus! This was not happening! Why did I have to get pregnant now? This was the worst timing ever! My husband and I are trying to get back on track. I don't trust him, and I don't think he trusts me. All this emotional turmoil, the ups and downs in our relationship, the abuse of all kinds, and now I'm pregnant! This didn't seem like the marriage I had been praying for. Dr. Harrison gave me the instructions and information to my OBGYN. I now know how to follow up with them. I left his office, still shocked.

I immediately told my husband that I was pregnant. I went to his job to tell him to his face. His reaction was what I expected. On the one hand, he was happy. On the other hand, he questioned if it was his, hell, me too. Admitting my mistakes and shortcomings is not something I have had too much of a problem doing. You don't need to inform everyone about your business, only the people it affects. So, being upfront about things was important to me.

This was not something I was going to pretend didn't exist. My child's paternity was in question. With it being in question, my husband was leaning more towards me having an abortion. It made sense, right? If there was any small amount of doubt about the paternity, then we should abort the baby and start over, right? My Dad even thought I should get an abortion. With all the drama in our marriage, he figured it would be better not to bring a baby into this mess. There was one BIG problem with the whole idea of having an abortion: I couldn't. WHY?

When I was around 18 years old, I lay on a cold table, with tears rolling down my face, having an abortion. At that very moment, I made a promise that if God ever blessed me to get pregnant again, I would never (ever) have another abortion, no matter the circumstance.

Here I am in the most uncomfortable, inconvenient situation, pregnant again! Yes, my marriage was online. People were going to talk about me, maybe even disown my child and me, but I had made a promise to my Heavenly Father that I could not break. To me, the answer was simple: my GOD blessed me. He loved me enough to forgive and give me another chance to bring life into the world. So my only response was YES, I will birth my baby! I didn't want an abortion, no matter the surrounding circumstances. Besides, what would this do for my blooming relationship with God? How could God ever trust my word if I break it now? How GOD receives my prayers and promises to HIM matters to me. It can be one of the things that keeps our prayers from being answered. I wasn't breaking the covenant I cut with GOD for no one! I made my decision: I'm not having an abortion!

After telling my husband I was going to keep my baby, all hell broke out. Of course, my husband put me and our baby on the back burner, at least behind closed doors. In public, he was happy that I was pregnant, but at home, he could care less. My husband would come home from work, shit, shower, shave, and be out the door to go galivant with whomever he chooses for the evening. Every day was the same routine.

My family wasn't much better. My Mom and sister are like, you should leave him, like right now. My Dad said I should have had the abortion because it would have made things smoother between me and my husband, and we could've started over and just tried for another baby. Also, my Father stated that he didn't know if he could be part of my child's life if my husband were not the Father of my child. Now, this threw my mental clarity off balance because my child was 100% my DNA. I didn't understand this "stance" from my earthly Father, but I didn't argue with any of this.

During my pregnancy, I was on bed rest in my first trimester. It was going to be a challenge for me to carry my baby full term. Therefore, I had to tune out everything around me and focus on the purpose, the plan, and the vision to deliver my baby healthy.

I knew my Mom and sister meant well, but as I told them, I would put more stress on the baby trying to up and leave my husband right now. I wanted my baby born with all her fingers and toes and without nervous conditions. Therefore, I would stay put and endure the verbal, mental, and blatant disrespect from my husband.

My earthly Father didn't understand my position. He was confused when I explained my agreement with GOD; he couldn't comprehend my reasoning. To my earthly Father, breaking my promise to GOD wouldn't have been a big deal. GOD would understand if I had to break my word. Let's say I wasn't willing to find out. Overall, it looked like hell on the outside, but it was one of the many times GOD truly blessed me on the inside with my baby. I couldn't go anywhere except to the doctor's office once a week, which gave me a lot of time to talk and pray to GOD. I prayed over my baby in my stomach every day. I asked GOD to put certain ingredients in my child and thanked HIM for it. I built my relationship with GOD so much during this time, and this is how I kept my peace within myself, my mind, my patience, and my tongue. That's right; I didn't bother to check my husband about his activities. My focus was on the promise I made with God and keeping it.

Memorial Day weekend is when I broke my silence and confronted my husband regarding a text message I saw on his phone from a woman telling him she "loved every inch of him last night." That was the same weekend I went into labor.

After an eventful trip to the hospital and 33 ½ hours of labor, Kayla was finally born! It had been a long, rough ride. I stayed sick the entire pregnancy. I was rushed to the hospital at almost five months pregnant because Kayla was trying to come out prematurely. At that time, the doctors put me on liquids-only medication to stop the contractions and an IV for two weeks. NO FOOD! I thought they were trying to kill me (LOL). Let's not forget that they performed an amniocentesis, where they stuck this huge needle in my stomach in order to pull amniotic fluid from my womb to make sure Kayla was not in distress. Not to mention, this needle had to enter my womb without penetrating my child.

I had an allergic reaction to the codeine they gave me, and they shot Kayla full of steroids to try to help her develop a little faster, just in case she was born right then. Well, Kyla waited not too long after that to make her grand entrance into this world. She was born two months premature at 5 pounds 11 ounces, 21.5 inches long, born with a touch of Jaundice, but she was beautiful!!! She spent the first two weeks of her life in the NICU unit. I visited her every day for as long as the doctors let me stay. I was in love with Kyla when she was in my womb, but meeting her in person was indescribable. The birth of my daughter changed everything for me.

Now that I wasn't pregnant, it was time to get things in order; believe me, everything was complete chaos. This man, my husband, had not paid the mortgage, barely a bill, nothing! I mean nothing! Our house and two investment property mortgages were behind, my car note was past due, utility bills were behind, and the over $30,000 he and I had in our savings was gone. I couldn't believe I was stupid enough to think he would hold me down. You know, take care of business! He didn't put anything into making all this happen for us like I did, so why would he care about it? Yes, this showed me how much he truly cared, or should I say he didn't care.

My husband looked at me and stated, "You care so much about your credit. You fix this. Call your Daddy. You'll fix this between the two of you and put my stuff back in order." I was livid! My husband did this because he figured when I got on my feet, I would grind up to fix all this??!!! Really!?!

That was not about to happen, not anymore! I was ready to let this go but was torn between staying and leaving. I grew up in a two-parent household, and that meant something to me to have my child raised by both her biological parents. I should do everything I could to keep us together, right? I should endure as much of his foolishness and disrespect as I could withstand to keep my daughter attached to her Father so she will have the privilege of being raised by both of us, right? Those were my thoughts until…

It had been a good day. It was Friday evening, and my husband was preparing to go out like usual—no big deal. Kayla and I will be home together, getting to know each other and loving on one another.

I mistakenly asked him where he was going, with whom, and how long he would be gone. I mean, why are we pretending he's not cheating with other women and living a double life? My questions sent him into defense mode because he got upset with me and started yelling. I'm trying not to yell back at him because I'm standing in the living room with Kayla on my chest. I told him I didn't care what he did; I was just asking.

Remember, I'm not a soft-spoken woman, so these comments came with an attitude and some base in my voice. As soon as I finished my sentence, he marched up to me and slapped me with a backhand right across my face, hard! To the point I almost dropped Kayla!!! Usually, he would hit me, and I would hit back, but this time was different. I'm a mother and must set a better example, and a better atmosphere for my child, so this shit wasn't going to happen anymore.

The fact that I could have dropped my newborn baby on this wooden floor in my living room enraged me! I didn't make a move right then and there. Instead, I walked away with my face burning and put Kayla down. I did not utter one word after that. He continued to get ready, and I watched.

Later, when he came home that evening, everything appeared fine. He took off his clothes as usual and got into bed. While he was sleeping, I was contemplating how I was going to kill him. I seriously wanted to slit his throat! This man doesn't even have enough respect for me or my baby to hit me while I'm holding her!! In my mind, it was either him or me! And it wasn't going to be me.

I sat looking at him with a knife in my hand all night. I thank God for the Holy Spirit because that is what saved my life and my husband's. The Holy Spirit told me this was not the way to go, and killing him would not solve anything. Not to mention, my baby girl would be without a mother or a father, and the devil would have gotten his way.

Now, as I was coming to this realization, my husband was waking up and saw me sitting in a chair, with a knife in my hand, on his side of the bed. Of course, this startled him a bit, but I didn't care. When he opened his eyes, I told him where I stood. I told him he should move out of the house for a while to give us some time to try and rebuild our marriage because, at this rate, I was going to kill him. I expressed to him that it took everything I had in me not to kill him in his sleep. I sat up all night trying to figure out the right way to slit your throat. This present environment wasn't healthy for anyone. After a second of assessing the seriousness of the situation, he agreed to move out.

I immediately helped him find a place to go, but he didn't know I was "helping" him. I found a perfect 1-bedroom apartment for him that was affordable and still centrally located to everything. Believe it or not, he was rather excited to move. My husband thought he would live as a bachelor and then come to the house to be the "family man" with a loving wife and child. It was easy for me to sell him on the idea that we needed to separate to work on our marriage. If he knew me at all, he would have known I'm not even cut that way. I don't believe in separating (in order) to stay together, but he never paid that much attention.

Once my husband moved out, I had law enforcement serve him with a restraining order. My marriage wasn't entirely over, but I could see my healing begin. I was able to file for divorce, move out of the house, and start over. I had to forgive myself for my poor decisions and the valuable time I thought I wasted. Yes, I thought, as for my poor decisions, they made me a wiser woman. Those decisions helped me to understand the value of a good man, the true meaning of healthy communication, and the pure way to appreciate love.

I found the balance in loving myself and others without depleting everything I had to offer. Reflecting on this trauma-filled time in my life, I am grateful and humbled that God felt I was strong enough to overcome my adversities. This experience didn't allow me to turn away from love. Instead, it increased my faith that God has a bigger plan for me. This experience helped grow my faith and relationship with God. It made me understand that I am stronger and more empowering than I believe I am. Against all odds, I still grew, thrived, and prospered in all areas of my life. Achieving my vision hasn't been easy, and believe me, there are still areas that need improvement, but I always leave room for growth. I'm married to my vision and purpose. No matter what happens, I will stay rooted in the word of God and not get discouraged if the plan changes, for ALL things work for my good.

With grace and humility, ladies, you must survive to thrive if only you believe. I encourage you to reread my story and, most importantly, reread the part about me asking for help from my girlfriends when I decided to move out. Lean not unto your understanding. There is help for you!

Sherri C Pickett

CHAPTER FIVE
NAVIGATING BULLYING
PATHWAYS TO STRENGTH
AND HEALING
ANNE KRISTINE AKSNES (NETHERLANDS)

<u>INTRODUCTION</u>

Dear Mother's,

I write these words with a heart overflowing with warmth, love, and unwavering support for you. As I embark on this journey of sharing some of my experiences and insights, I cannot help but feel a deep sense of empathy and understanding for the trials and tribulations you face as the mother of a child who is being bullied.

I know firsthand the pain, anguish, and loneliness that can consume a mother's heart when her precious child becomes a target of bullying. I, too, have walked the path you now find yourself on. I have felt the sting of unkind words, the weight of indifference, and the relentless torment that can overshadow a child's spirit. I experienced being bullied as a child, and my beloved child experienced bullying for years. I have felt the despair and fear of not being able to protect my child. But most importantly, I have conquered those dark moments, emerging stronger, wiser, and ready to extend my hand to you in support.

This chapter is born out of a burning desire (within me) to offer hope, knowledge, and solace to mothers (who find themselves) grappling with the overwhelming challenge of navigating their child through the treacherous waters of bullying. It is a testament to our unwavering love for our children, an ode to the fierce protectiveness that dwells within our souls, and a reminder that we are never alone in this battle.

Through my own personal journey, I have come to understand that the path of a bullied child is not one tread solely by them but also by their mothers, shoulder to shoulder, hand in hand. We are the guardians of their dreams, the warriors of their happiness, and the bearers of their burdens. Together, we can empower ourselves with the knowledge to navigate the stormy seas of bullying. We can instill resilience and strength in our children and create a world where kindness triumphs over cruelty.

Within the pages of this chapter, you will find insights, knowledge, stories, and poetry crafted with the intention of guiding you toward a brighter tomorrow. I offer my own experiences and the wisdom I have gathered from experts, psychologists, and fellow mothers who have traversed this challenging terrain. Together, we will uncover the tools necessary to empower our children, build a supportive community, and stand tall against bullying.

Know that as you read these words, you are not alone. I stand beside you, holding your hand, offering a shoulder to lean on and a compassionate heart. This chapter is a testament to the love we share for our children, the strength we possess as mothers, and the unyielding hope that shines within us.

Let us embark on this journey together, armed with knowledge, fortified by love, and ready to face the challenges head-on. Remember, dear mother, you are not alone, and together, we can create a world where our children can thrive and not just survive from being burdened by the weight of bullying.

Once upon a time, in a small town nestled amidst rolling hills, there lived a loving mother named Sarah. Her world revolved around her son, David, a bright and compassionate young boy with a heart full of dreams. David had always been a source of joy and inspiration for Sarah, but one fateful day, her world came crashing down when he tearfully revealed that he was being bullied.

As the words escaped David's trembling lips, Sarah's heart shattered into a million pieces. Anguish consumed her, making her feel helpless and filled with an overwhelming sense of guilt. How could such cruelty exist in a world that she had tried so hard to shield him from? She knew that she had to find the strength within herself to help her son overcome this pain.

With determination in her eyes, Sarah embarked on a journey to reclaim her son's happiness. She sought guidance from wise counselors, who provided her with valuable tools to navigate the treacherous waters of bullying. Together, they devised a plan to empower David, to instill within him the belief that he was worthy of love, respect, and happiness.

The road to recovery was not an easy one. David's spirit had been bruised, his confidence shaken to its core. Each day was a battle, but Sarah refused to give up. She reminded him that he was not defined by the hurtful words or actions of others, and that she believed in him and supported him. She knew that he had the strength and resilience he needed within him.

Sarah encouraged David to express his emotions freely and find solace in his passions and hobbies. She enrolled him in art classes, where he discovered a newfound love for painting. Through the vibrant colors and strokes of his brush, David found an escape, a sanctuary where the pain could be transformed into something beautiful.

In time, David slowly blossomed. He discovered true friends who appreciated his kindness and gentle nature. With his mother's support and newfound friendships, David grew stronger with each passing day. Sarah watched with pride as her son began to stand tall, his spirit once again shining brightly. As time went by, he built strong friendships and had hobbies and a job he enjoyed. His life was meaningful and good.

Tears welled up in Sarah's eyes, and she was overwhelmed with gratitude for her son's resilience and the unwavering support they had received along his journey. The painful memories of bullying had transformed into a testament of triumph, a story of love and courage.

Together, they had conquered the darkness, emerging into a world where happiness and kindness prevailed.

And so, as the sun set over the rolling hills, Sarah and David walked side by side, grateful for the strength they had found within themselves and embracing the beauty that had emerged from the pain.

In order to effectively tackle the issue of bullying and support our children, it is crucial for us to have a clear understanding of what children (really) need. And when children are asked, their answer is clear.

<u>BUT WHAT EXACTLY CONSTITUTES BULLYING?</u>

Bullying is not simply a harmless part of growing up; it is a serious concern that can have detrimental effects on our children's well-being. It is essential to recognize that bullying encompasses a range of behaviors that involve an imbalance of power between the perpetrator and the victim. For the targeted children of bullying, these behaviors can be physical, verbal, or psychological, causing harm and distress.

The Norwegian government writes:

"A common, general definition of bullying is the following: A person is bullied when he or she, repeatedly and over a certain period, is exposed to negative actions from one or more other individuals (1). The definition also includes that the person being targeted has difficulty defending themselves."

(https://www.regjeringen.no/globalassets/upload/bld/mobbing/m obbing_i_frtismiljoene.pdf)

Erling Roland, a professor of educational psychology working at the National Center for Learning Environment and Behavioural Research at the University of Stavanger (Norway), has a definition that I think is good: Bullying is systematic physical or psychological violence from one or more together against one, who cannot defend themselves in the given situation (Roland, 2007; Roland & Vaaland, 2003).

An important element in the definition is the imbalance of power between the perpetrators and the person being bullied".

(https://www.uis.no/nb/laringsmiljosenteret/forskning/hva-er-mobbing#:~:text=Mobbing%20er%20systematisk%20fysisk%20eller,og%20den%20som%20blir%20mobbet.)

Bullying can manifest in different ways, each leaving its own emotional and psychological scars on our children. **Physical bullying** involves aggressive actions such as hitting, pushing, or stealing their belongings. **Verbal bullying** includes name-calling, insults, or spreading rumors. **Psychological bullying** is often more subtle and may involve exclusion, manipulation, or cyberbullying through social media platforms.

In today's digital age, cyberbullying has become a prevalent form of harassment. It occurs when individuals use technology, such as social media or messaging apps, to intimidate, threaten, or humiliate others. **Cyberbullying** can be particularly distressing as it invades our children's safe spaces, reaching them wherever they are, making it crucial for mothers to be vigilant and knowledgeable about online interactions.

Defining bullying is the first step in empowering us to support our children effectively. By understanding the various forms of bullying, including physical, verbal, psychological, and cyberbullying, we can equip ourselves with the knowledge needed to address this issue head-on. Recognizing the signs, understanding the impact, and drawing the line between normal conflicts and bullying behaviors will enable us to navigate our child's bullying experience with confidence and determination. Together, we can rise above and create a safe and nurturing environment for our children.

RECOGNIZING THE SIGNS OF BULLYING

As mothers, one of the most challenging experiences we can face is witnessing our child being bullied. It can be heartbreaking to see them suffer, and we often feel helpless and unsure of how to support them. However, by being aware of the signs of bullying, we can take the first step towards understanding and addressing this issue.

First and foremost, it is essential to recognize the behavioral changes in our children. If your child suddenly becomes withdrawn, anxious, or starts avoiding certain places or people, it could be a sign that they are being bullied. They might also exhibit changes in their sleeping or eating patterns, experience frequent nightmares, or complain of physical ailments like headaches or stomachaches without any medical cause. It is important to pay attention to these shifts in behavior and take them seriously.

Another sign to look out for is a decline in academic performance. Bullied children often struggle to concentrate or may no longer enjoy activities they once loved. They may even start skipping school to avoid their tormentors. By understanding the connection between bullying and academic performance, we can intervene and provide the necessary support to help our children regain their confidence and love for learning.

Social isolation is another red flag that indicates bullying. If your child suddenly loses interest in spending time with friends or participating in social activities, it could be a sign that they feel excluded or targeted by their peers. Bullies often aim to isolate their victims, making them feel alone and vulnerable. As mothers, we can foster open communication and encourage our children to share their experiences with us, their teachers, or a trusted adult.

Lastly, but equally important, we must be vigilant about unexplained physical injuries or damaged belongings. Bruises, cuts, torn clothing, or missing personal items can all point toward bullying. If your child frequently comes home with such marks or their belongings are consistently damaged, it is crucial to investigate the situation further and take appropriate action.

Recognizing the signs of bullying is the first step in supporting our children through this challenging experience. By staying attentive and observant, we can provide them with the love, empathy, and guidance they need to overcome bullying and rise above it.

THE FIRST STEPS TOWARD HEALING

<u>Listening and validating your child's feelings and experiences:</u>

A short story: Emily's Echo

Emily, a bright and artistic 10-year-old, was bullied relentlessly at school. Her mother, noticing the change in her once vibrant daughter, sat down with her, offering a safe space to share her pain. Through tears, Emily spoke of her loneliness and fear. Her mother listened, her heart breaking, but her presence and validation became Emily's first step toward healing. Together, they began navigating the path to recovery, reinforcing the power of a mother's understanding and support.

Bullying is an ordeal that can leave deep imprints on a child's soul. It's a storm that, unfortunately, too many children navigate through.

Megan Meier's heart-wrenching words to her mother, "I thought you were supposed to be on my side," really hit me as I heard her mother's testimony. Megan's plea underscores children's profound need for their mother's unconditional love and support during such tumultuous times.

Remember, it's not about finding a quick fix; it's about understanding, supporting, and empowering your child through their healing journey. Your role is pivotal—children who are bullied say the most critical support comes from their mothers, who listen, believe, validate their feelings, and stand firmly by their side. A large study by the Megan Meier Foundation, born from a heart-wrenching story of loss, confirms this.

STRATEGIES FOR SUPPORTING YOUR CHILD

<u>Listen with your heart:</u>

The first step in supporting your child is to listen—truly listen. Create a safe and loving space where your child feels comfortable sharing their feelings without fear of judgment or dismissal. It's in these moments of vulnerability that your empathy becomes their haven. By validating their feelings, you acknowledge their pain, letting them know it's okay to feel scared, hurt, or angry. This simple act of listening can be incredibly healing.

TOOLS FOR BUILDING TRUST

Active listening is essential in building trust and understanding with your child. When your child shares their bullying experience, listening attentively without interrupting or passing judgment is important. Ensure you are fully present and engaged, giving them your undivided attention. Maintain eye contact, nod, and encourage them to express their emotions and thoughts freely. By actively listening, you convey to your child that their feelings and experiences are valid, fostering a deeper bond between you and your child.

Communication is a two-way street, and it is vital to encourage open dialogue with your child. Create a safe space where they feel comfortable sharing their concerns, fears, and anxieties. Avoid dismissing or trivializing their emotions, as this can discourage them from further communication. Instead, validate their feelings, empathize with their pain, and reassure them that you are there to support them unconditionally.

Ask open-ended questions to encourage your child to elaborate on their experiences. Doing so can give you a deeper understanding of the situation and provide targeted assistance. Avoid interrogating or pressuring them for information, as this may cause them to withdraw. Patience is another critical tool when discussing bullying with your child. Allow them to share at their own pace, and be prepared to offer comfort and reassurance when needed.

USE UNCONDITIONAL LOVE AS A SHIELD

Your unconditional love is the most potent shield against the slings and arrows of bullying. The silent whisper in your child's heart says, "I am loved, I am valued, no matter what." This unwavering support fosters resilience, empowering your child to stand tall amidst adversity. Let them know, through words and actions, that your love is not contingent upon grades, achievements, or the opinions of others.

ADVOCACY: STANDING IN THEIR CORNER

Being on your child's side means more than just emotional support; it's about advocacy. Work with them to develop strategies to address the bullying, whether through direct communication with the school, seeking professional guidance, or empowering them with tools for resilience. Your involvement 'sends a powerful message' that your child is not alone in this battle.

EQUIP YOUR CHILD WITH TOOLS FOR RESILIENCE

Empower your child with tools for resilience. Teach them about the power of positive self-talk, the importance of surrounding themselves with supportive friends, and the value of engaging in activities that boost their self-esteem. Please encourage them to express their feelings through art, music, or writing, transforming pain into something beautiful and cathartic.

Teach your child the importance of self-care and self-compassion. Help them discover their strengths and talents, as these will serve as sources of resilience during challenging times. Praise their efforts and celebrate their achievements, no matter how small, to boost their self-esteem.

THE HEALING POWER OF TOGETHERNESS

Spend quality time together doing activities that foster connection and joy. Whether it's a walk in nature, baking cookies, or simply cuddling up with a good book, these moments of togetherness are healing balm to a troubled heart. They remind your child of the beauty and love in the world beyond the pain of bullying, and it will make them stronger.

ENCOURAGING HEALTHY COPING MECHANISMS

Teaching your child healthy ways to manage stress and emotions is another vital aspect of coping with bullying. Please encourage them to engage in activities that bring them joy and boost their self-confidence—Ranging from pursuing hobbies, participating in sports, or joining clubs and organizations where they can connect with like-minded individuals.

Mindfulness and relaxation techniques can also be incredibly beneficial. Teach your child deep breathing exercises or meditation to help them find inner calm and manage their anxiety. These practices can give them a sense of control and help them build resilience in the face of adversity. It's also healthy for their mental health and strengthens their psychological immune defense.

Furthermore, encourage your child to seek support from trusted adults, such as teachers, school counselors, or mentors. These individuals can provide guidance, offer solutions, and advocate for your child's well-being within the school community. Remind your child that asking for help is not a sign of weakness but a courageous step toward finding a resolution.

A JOURNEY OF GROWTH

Finally, frame this experience as a journey of growth. While it's a path no one would choose, it can lead to profound personal development. Together, you can discover lessons in empathy, strength, and the importance of being authentic and appreciate oneself and others. These are the silver linings, the hidden gifts in a problematic situation.

And remember, as mothers, we must model healthy coping mechanisms ourselves. Our children look up to us for guidance and support. Show them how to handle difficult emotions and stressful situations by practicing self-care, seeking support when needed, and maintaining a positive mindset.

Navigating your child's bullying experience can be overwhelming. However, by encouraging healthy coping mechanisms, you empower yourself and your child to rise above the challenges.

<u>CONCLUSION</u>

Mother, you play a crucial role in your child's life. Your love, support, and guidance are fundamental in shaping their self-esteem, resilience, and overall well-being. When your child is experiencing bullying, it is normal to feel overwhelmed, helpless, and even angry. However, it is important to remember that you are not alone. By arming yourself with knowledge and adopting effective strategies, you can become a powerful advocate for your child.

Throughout this chapter, we have discussed various aspects of bullying, including its different forms, signs to look out for, and what your child needs from you when bullied. We have explored the importance of open communication with your child and the significance of teaching your child coping mechanisms to deal with bullying.

It is time to bring all these pieces together and empower you, the mother, to take charge of the situation. Being proactive and involved as a loving, caring mother can create a safe and supportive environment for your child. This involves staying informed about your child's experiences, maintaining open lines of communication, and working collaboratively with school personnel to address the issue.

Remember, empowerment starts with self-care. As a mother, it is essential to prioritize your own well-being. Mothers, you will be better equipped to support your child effectively by taking care of yourself. Seek support from other parents, professionals, or support groups who can offer guidance and understanding. Listening to bullying experiences from other children in support groups can also be used as an effective tool for your child.

<u>**FINAL WORDS OF ENCOURAGEMENT**</u>

I want to assure you that you have the strength and capability to rise above the challenges of your child's bullying experience. By empowering yourself, you will empower your child to navigate this difficult journey with resilience and courage. Together, we can create a world where bullying has no place. We can create a world where every child can thrive, not just survive.

You are not alone, and I am here to support you every step of the way. Remember, you are a powerful force for change. Trust in your abilities, trust in your child, and together, we will rise above.

With all my love,

Anne

P.S. Remember, in the darkest times, your love is your child's brightest beacon. Keep shining, dear mother. You are their hero.

LIGHT WITHIN

In the shadows where whispers dwell,
Where courage falls, and fears swell,
You're not alone, though it's hard to tell,
In the echoes of your silent yell.
Through the storm, a light does shine,
It's yours to claim this life divine.
The voices are cruel; let them not define,
The strength within, let it brightly align.
When the world seems cold and vast,
Remember, this pain will not last.
From the ashes of the past,
A warrior emerges, unsurpassed.
Stand tall against the gale,
With every step, you will prevail.
Your spirit, let it set sail,
Against the wind, you will not fail.
Rise up, rise against the tide,
With hope and courage as your guide.
Let your heart be your fearless ride,
In yourself, deeply confide.
So hold on to the light within,
Let your journey now begin.
With hope and courage, you will win,
In the symphony of life, let your song spin.

-   By Anne Kristine Aksnes

ABOUT THE AUTHOR

ANNE KRISTINE AKENES

The road to recovery from bullying is a journey of a thousand steps, filled with challenges and triumphs. As a mother, your love, understanding, and support are the most powerful weapons in your arsenal. Embrace them, and step bravely forward with your child into a future where the light of your collective strength and resilience dispels the shadows of bullying.

Remember, you are good enough, and your child needs your love.

Anne Kristine Akenes

CHAPTER SIX
IF GOD WOULD NOT LET ME DIE
I HAD TO LEARN HOW TO LIVE
TRACY WHITT, CARC (USA)

HUMBLE BEGINNINGS

I grew up in a small town in East Tennessee. We were poor and didn't have much at all, but somehow, we always made it to church. We didn't even have running water in our home until we moved at age eleven. My Dad, a deacon in the church, was Pentecostal in faith and very strict. I had to wear a dress (every day), and I wasn't allowed to wear makeup or jewelry; we couldn't even braid our hair.

No music was allowed except for gospel and a little bit of country. My grandfather was also a preacher. He didn't have a television in the nineties, and we (definitely) weren't allowed to watch mainstream movies. Nevertheless, I'm so thankful now for how I was raised. When I hit rock bottom, I knew that I could look up and my help would come from the Lord.

Life was tough, but wasn't everyone's life tumultuous somehow? All I knew was that I thought I didn't fit in, no matter how hard I tried. I always had the feeling that I was homesick. Homesick for a place where there was love and peace. I made it my goal to find this place. Little did I know how hard this would be.

I went through quite a few things as a child, including different types of abuse. I'm sure there are more things that I can't remember that my mind has repressed to save my sanity. I know now that my coping mechanism was dissociation, and this led me to have an addictive personality as well. I was addicted to unwanted behavior patterns – anything that took my mind away from reality. During these dark days, this was where I needed to be. At least, that's what I was thinking.

At first, I was addicted to positive things, like making good grades. I was obsessed with the clothes I wore (that was rather hard for a teenager from a poverty-stricken family). If I could only escape my (little) small town and go somewhere better, life would be amazing, and I could finally be the person I was meant to be.

Even though I was an excellent student, I quit high school at age sixteen, enrolled in a Job Corps center, and got my GED from North Carolina. I promptly started computer courses while waiting to attend a small community college that next semester. I planned to go to college early and begin a new life. Meanwhile, my fellow students had other plans-apparently, I did too! I started smoking cigarettes and marijuana. I began drinking alcohol and lost my virginity all in one week. It was like the floodgates had opened, and I had all these new things to try. This was just the beginning of my cycle of addiction. I lost my opportunity to go to college and was quickly sent home. I had my GED, so the next step was to find a job. I soon was able to purchase a car.

After this, I dabbled in a few drugs and a little alcohol here and there, but nothing major. Suddenly, depression set in. No matter what I did or where I was, I never felt like I belonged. It was so much more than not fitting in; I didn't want to be on earth. I felt like if I prayed long and hard and had enough faith, God would come back, get me, and take me back home. Feeling this way led to me being depressed and anxiety-ridden throughout my teenage years. My dream of a better life would have to wait for now.

At age twenty, I finally got my chance to leave home. I liked to party with my friends, but I was pretty much a functional addict. One day, at age twenty-five, that all changed. Until then, I had stayed with friends or my boyfriend but decided it was time to strike out on my own. I got my very own little apartment, was working a couple blocks away, and was working on getting myself a car so that I would be (totally) self-sufficient. I'd always walk down to the nearby gas station every Sunday to call my Mom & Dad to let them know I was okay and update them about my week and plans.

I guess the guy had been watching me because he knew no one else was in my apartment. He pulled up behind me to ask for directions. I told him what he wanted to know. Then I turned to put my key in the door. When I turned the key and opened the door, he was behind me and pushed me into my apartment. He started to beat me, hitting me in my head and my face. He told me not to scream because no one would hear me. I thought, "My God, he is right!" (Most people who lived in that apartment building were always gone on the weekend, but how did he know that?)

Then I thought (to myself), if I'm going to survive this, I will cooperate and do whatever he asks me to do. This only made him angry; he wanted me to fight back and be terrified! I'll skip all the details, but when he got done beating me and raping me, I thought he was going to kill me. He didn't. He said that I was a worthless piece of 'white trash' and that if I told anyone what he did, they wouldn't believe me. Even now, I can't remember his face (I think my mind repressed this memory because if I had remembered it, I would've been looking for him in every face I saw), but I did remember it at the moment, *and* what his car looked like. He was sentenced to twenty years in the Alabama State Prison, serving over eighteen years. He got out in March of 2018.

On top of depression and an addictive personality, I now had PTSD. My drug use spiraled out of control. I had to sleep with a loaded gun. I couldn't and wouldn't live by myself anymore. I started having suicidal ideation. I still didn't want to be in Alabama. After the trial, I decided to move back home. Some days were good, and some were bad, but I was back in Tennessee with my family. I'm glad I came back when I did because my father passed away that same year at age fifty-eight.

My neighbor, who became my husband, helped me through the grieving process. But he had his (own) life lessons to teach me. We drank and did whatever drugs we could get. He had his (own) demons to fight. My husband ended up putting me through mental and emotional abuse as well. Before marriage, we would play music, sing, and attend concerts. We always had friends over to party with us, but after we got married, all that was out. I couldn't go anywhere besides work or to my family's house. In between all this, I decided to go to college and become the first person in my family to do so. When I began college, my marriage ended. I tried to make my marriage work because of how I was raised. When you get married, there is no such thing as divorce; it's until death do you part. This caused me a lot of shame and grief because I felt like a failure, but I knew I didn't want to be unhappy for the rest of my Life.

While in college, I met my second husband. I had stopped doing *all drugs* because he was fresh out of the Army and didn't approve of drugs. I didn't mention anything about (being the addict) that I (really) was. Drinking was okay with him, so guess what? What did I get good at? Drinking, and so did my second husband. We were successful for a while. I was attending college, and we had our own property management business. We moved to Kentucky for his job, and I started selling cars full-time. We had the American dream. The urge to do drugs was great, but I could drown out that feeling with alcohol. There was one feeling that was always on my mind. At this point in my life, I wanted to be a mother. I was 30 years old, in my second marriage, and still had no children.

Was this God's punishment for me since I didn't appreciate life and wanted to go back to heaven? Or that I'd messed up my own life so badly that I didn't deserve or couldn't handle another life that required me to be responsible? Either way, I prayed every day to become a mother. Finally, the day came, at age thirty-two, I had my son, Ethan. That was the only time ever in my adult life that I had abstained from drugs *AND* alcohol.

 Life was good for a while, and I thought I had finally succeeded! We bought a house, I had a brand-new Jeep, and I enjoyed life as a mother! But it wasn't going to last. The battlefield was in my mind, and I had no idea how to overcome it. I slowly started drinking again, but what changed was when I went to the dentist for a root canal. Percocet 10s. I soon couldn't function without them. All the while, my husband was drinking more and more and soon started even drinking on his lunch hour to make it through the day. Life spiraled downward, and I was about to lose my 'American dream.' In my husband's eyes, I couldn't do anything right anymore and faced constant criticism.

One day, right before Christmas, he left Ethan and me without any money and went to Tennessee. He left us there in that big house all alone for Christmas. I suspected he was cheating on me, but soon, I would see the proof with my very own eyes on

Facebook. Nothing was the same. After that, he tried to come back and reconcile. It didn't work, and I couldn't get those pictures out of my head.

We separated, and I moved to an apartment a couple blocks down the street. I thought....okay, this is not good, but I can get through it, and I prepared to take care of Ethan, who had just been diagnosed with Asperger's Syndrome on the autism spectrum while going through a lengthy court battle for divorce. I needed relief from all the trauma, hurt, and disappointment I was facing, so I turned to the only thing I knew that I thought would help...pharmaceuticals. I was already getting them from my dentist, but soon, that wasn't enough.

I found a friend who could supply all my needs, and he was the exact opposite of my husband. It wasn't long before we started dating, about six months after I moved out alone. This move would change my life forever. He was really into some hard drugs, but after all I'd been through, I didn't care about that, and he seemed like the perfect escape from my failure in life. He was (really, really) good to Ethan and me. He would ensure we had everything we needed and do anything for us. I wouldn't let him move in with me, but he would spend the night sometimes.

One day, after him being gone all day drinking and doing cocaine, he came over to spend the night. I thought this would be my last night on earth. I had just found out I was pregnant about a month before, and I was already 4 ½ months along. I wasn't being cautious about getting pregnant because it had been so hard for me to get pregnant the first time. My phone rang, and I didn't recognize the number, so I just let it ring.

By not answering, this enraged him more, and he thought I had something to hide and immediately started punching my face. He let up for a second. I was dazed. Where did that come from? He'd never hit me before. As soon as I turned to look at his eyes, he started choking me out. When I looked at him, it was like looking at an empty shell of a man. I don't think he even knew what he was doing. My abuse lasted six hours. He would choke me and beat my head and my face over & over again. At one point, I asked him to let me smoke a cigarette, and he lit it and put it out on my face. Then he tore the rest of the pack up. His action saved us (myself, Ethan, and the child I was carrying). I was wondering how I could get away the whole time. It was January in Kentucky, and snow and ice covered the ground. Ethan was asleep on the couch (thank God he didn't see any of this!). And the whole time, I had to protect the child inside me.

I had a loaded .38 on top of my wardrobe, and he knew it. If I even looked up that way, he would beat me harder. So many times, he choked me out until I felt life seeping out of my body. I just kept praying that God would give me the strength to endure. He wouldn't just be killing me, but the baby inside of me and Ethan would be without his mother. I had to survive! Finally, the drugs started to wear off, and he got tired. He laid down on my bed and told me to lie beside him. I was so scared of being beaten and choked out again that I lay perfectly still beside him. Time seemed like it stopped, but I didn't move, and he finally woke up and wanted a cigarette.

He says, "Take me to the store." I got Ethan ready to go, and we all got in the car to go to the store. When he exited the vehicle and entered the store, I backed out of the parking lot and left him there. I couldn't go to the police. He had shown me many times how he had two social security numbers and his brother was DEA (Drug Enforcement Agent) and would promptly get him out of any drug-related charges. It may have been just a ruse, but I believed him because I knew what he was doing and what he was capable of doing.

I went to the last place he thought I'd go....to my former home, which I still owned (and still do, to this day). I parked my car in the garage, shut it off, and knocked on the door. I'll never forget my ex's face when he saw me...I hadn't had a chance to look at myself, but when he saw my face, he started screaming, "What happened? What happened? Who did this to you?" My face was swollen and bruised in every area possible, and my neck from my collarbone up was just one continuous bruise.

God wasn't ready to let me go, and I was stronger than ever. We made it; the three of us survived: me, Ethan, and the unborn child I was carrying. It took him four days to get there after I called my brother in Tennessee to come get us. He came with a short-bed Chevy truck and a trailer, and we crammed all I had to show for twenty years of my life in it. Everything I owned was now on the back of a truck, stacked in my car, and headed for Tennessee.

I found myself single, pregnant, along with a three-year-old who has special needs, with nowhere to go except my mother's house. I couldn't take all my things to my mom's, so my brother very courteously said I could store all my stuff in his garage. "No worries, as soon as you get back on your feet and get a place, you can come back and get your things," he said.

I'm holding on, trying to be strong, taking care of Ethan and my pregnant self the best I can so I can have my baby and get back on my feet. Finally, one early morning, about 2 am, I went into labor, and I didn't have anyone to take me to the hospital. I called 911, and the ambulance took me to the hospital. Every time I had a contraction, Colton's heart rate would go down (this was very dangerous). The doctors came in rushing around, getting things ready for an emergency C-section. I woke up and had a healthy baby boy. I, on the other hand, was in intense pain! My pain was worse than the contractions, and that wasn't good. I looked at my stomach, which had a purple spot that kept getting bigger and bigger. I was bleeding internally. I was in and out of consciousness because the doctors put me on a morphine drip and monitored the growing spot on my stomach.

I woke up at one point and saw my Dad praying at the end of my bed. Typically, this wouldn't have been unusual, but my Dad passed away in 2000, and this was in 2011. Right after that, a tornado came through. The hospital staff moved all the patients into the hallway and all the babies into the nursery, with no outside windows. Was that God coming through? I don't know, but I chose to think it was. After that, the spot on my stomach stopped growing, and the pain eased up. Once again, we had survived. Colton, Ethan, and I were saved once again.

I tried to provide my kids the best life possible, but this was challenging. I still had mental issues that were worse after what Colton's father had done to me and all the other trauma I had gone through before that.

I finally got an apartment for me and my kids. I returned to get my furniture and everything I owned from my brother's house. To my surprise, nothing was left. It was all gone, and he had nothing to say about why. He kept, sold, or threw away everything I owned. Losing everything you own except what you can carry with you is very traumatizing in itself.

My problems with my brother happened around the same time I started having back trouble and lots of pain, so I started seeing a spine specialist. I found out I had scoliosis and a condition called spondylolisthesis (it's where the vertebrae in your back are out of alignment, and it causes the discs to protrude onto your spinal cord). It eventually causes your legs to feel (like they are) asleep, and you lose function. I started going to a pain clinic. With my condition, they loaded me up with all kinds of pain medication. My addictions kicked in full force once again.

One day, I was driving around running errands. I lost my phone in my car and pulled over to find it. The police pulled into the parking lot and charged me with Public Intoxication for taking my prescribed medication. They took my kids away from me. I fully complied with all their demands. I took the random drug tests, the parenting, and A&D classes, plus I attended all the meetings they had me go to for ninety days straight. I was two days away from getting my children back for a 90-day trial period. If nothing went wrong, I would get them back permanently. When officials showed up to do a pill count, I was a couple of pills short. They told me I'd never get my kids back if they had anything to do with it. I was ordered to start the process all over again.

Being denied custody of my children broke my heart. After everything I did to get them back, they told me I (still) wasn't good enough to be a mother! I wasn't going to be able to see my kids for a while. I was a total failure as a mother, and they (the system) weren't going to give me my kids back!

I became suicidal, and I started taking more and more pills to ease the pain of not being able to see my kids. One night, I was in deep despair; I decided that if I couldn't be a mother to my kids, I might as well die. I went and got a point and got my friend to show me how to use it. I went back home, opened my bottle, and started doing five oxycodone 30s at a time (this is all that would fit on the spoon). I did five, then five more until I had done twenty. I figured I would go to sleep and be out of this cold, cruel world forever.

About two hours later, I woke up and was so angry that I had woken up! Why was I still alive?!? I'm trying to kill myself, and I couldn't even do that right! I reasoned that my body is immune to taking pain medication. If I (really) wanted to die, I'd have to take something I wasn't used to taking. About two weeks later, I found some totem poles. I bought all they had (totem poles are 2.5 mg Xanax, so it's like taking two and a half Xanax 10s). I had seventeen of them. One 10mg is enough to knock anyone out for a 12-hour sleep. I went to my apartment and took all of them. This time, I woke up in jail three days later, and when I woke up, I was cursing out the CO. Why, I don't know, but I was mad at the whole world! Why wouldn't God let me die?!? In my eyes, I was worthless, and if I wasn't fit to be a mother, then I wasn't fit to live!

After this, I didn't care what I did. **I put myself in the worst situations possible, hoping something terrible would happen and I'd get killed**. After all, didn't women get killed all the time by putting themselves in compromising situations? It was like I was protected everywhere I went: the trap houses, in bad neighborhoods with violence all around. I'd walk down the street at three in the morning, and nothing ever happened. I slept in my car, slept on people's couches, didn't take care of myself, and did as many drugs as I could get my hands on. I did get robbed a couple of times, but all that did was make me feel even worse. I wasn't paying my fines from court, so they took my driver's license. I kept getting pulled over and didn't have a license, so I was in and out of jail while the fines and court costs added up.

Finally, I caught a casual exchange charge that was a little more serious. I almost went to prison and would have if the lead investigator had not had to resign and, therefore, could not testify against me in court. I spent about three months in jail, got out on probation, and then got locked up again for probation violation. They sent me to rehab. I got out and immediately went and got high.

I was back on the wrong PATH again! About a year later, I pulled into a park with my friend to get high. The cops pulled in, and I got arrested. My car was impounded with everything I owned. Once again, I lost all my earthly possessions. I lost my car and everything in it. This was the insidious, vicious cycle I was on. I was hopeless with no way out and worthless in my own eyes, a miserable addict who had lost everything, including my children. I had hit absolutely rock bottom! I was in and out of jails and institutions. I don't know how many times I've been arrested or committed. The only thing left was death, and I couldn't manage to do that right! **Losing my freedom meant nothing. I was already a prisoner in a decrepit cell of my own making.**

PARADIGM SHIFT

This thought ran on a constant loop over and over in my mind: **If God would not let me die, I had to learn how to live.**

In jail, waiting to go to rehab again, I got down on my knees and asked the Lord to forgive me. I promised from then on **that I would live my life for Him**—the promises of Alcoholics Anonymous rang through my mind. I had read their literature many times throughout my stays at rehabs and attempts to get into and maintain recovery. Would God do for me what I could not do for myself? Would my whole attitude and outlook on life change? I had to try. I didn't have any other choice. With sincerity running through me, I promised my Life to God, and whatever happened had to be better than my miserable Life.

I didn't end up like this by failing morally or being a bad person. I was trying to survive in a cold, cruel world with a traumatized brain. I was hurting so badly from the emotional pain and had lost my connection to my Higher Power.

That was August 22nd, 2018. I finally got out of jail and was sent to a rehab center in Memphis. I was in shackles and handcuffs (yes, for the whole eight-hour drive, courtesy of the Hawkins County Hilton). When I left the rehabilitation center, they gave me a bus ticket back to my hometown. I knew for sure I couldn't go back to my hometown! I knew (for sure) it would be more of the same unending misery if I went back there.

The bus made its stop in Nashville, and I looked up and wondered what I was going to do. I had no plan. I got off in Nashville, TN, with a backpack and $5 to my name, and the bus departed without me. Something deep inside told me to get off there and try to make a whole new life, a fresh start. I was so scared! What would I do? How would I survive?

I remembered my promise to God and remembered His promise to me. Walking down the street in Nashville that first day, I kept saying, "I trust you, Lord, I trust you, Lord." Then I asked, "God, please send me an angel." I knew I needed help but didn't know a soul here. God sent one of his dearest, who had been through so much (in his life), to help me.

He stopped at the post office to check his mail and saw me looking up like I was lost and didn't know what to do. This was the (exact) moment I was praying to God to send me an angel, someone to help me. I told him my situation. He said, "Give me ten days." Ten days later, I had a place to live and a job.

Meanwhile, I stayed in a room at the Inn, a church-funded program for people experiencing homelessness in the heart of Nashville, near the Greyhound Bus Station at the beginning of 8th Avenue. Things started miraculously working out for me. I can see clearly now! A leap of faith and total surrender is the key to your empowerment. I had to make it. I was still alive for a reason, and I was determined to Find My Moment of Clarity.

Just when I needed it the most, I committed my life to the Father, God, my Higher Power. He was right there for me, holding my hand. I am living my life for God now. His will not mine! And remember, this is all just borrowed time. I should've been dead a long time ago, but God had a purpose for my life, and He has one for you too! I live my life for God daily, and only He knows when I will finally be allowed to return home (heaven).

God is no respecter of persons (Acts 10:34). What that means is what He will do for me, He will do for you! As the promises read in the AA Big book: "No matter how far down the scale you have gone, we will see how our experience can help others." (AA Big book p.83 – the promises). I have been fascinated by reading the promises throughout the years. This was one of the things I had read that planted a seed of hope in my mind. I didn't know how true they would become for me.

My life is (totally) different now. I have a place to live, and a nice vehicle, and my son Colton is back with me. I honestly do know a new freedom, a new happiness, and peace. I help people from all walks of life every day. As I began to understand How To Harness The Power of Purpose, He kept me, *preserved me*, and *WOULD NOT let me die!* I will live, not die, to help and serve others! Life can be Smoothie Time when your Higher Power holds your hand.

I knew I wanted to help people in this newly found freedom. I didn't know how to do this without a degree. I found a program of study that was life-changing for me and exactly what I needed to fulfill my purpose. I spent a lot of time working on myself, healing from the abuse and trauma, and developing a whole new skill set. **I am now a certified addictions and abuse recovery coach who earned some bonafide credentials; I am Tracy Whitt, CARC.** Not Tracy Whitt, hopeless addict. God is good. It's my dream to open up a recovery home to help others who are going through what I went through. If God can change my life, He can change anyone! I now know that all I went through was part of a bigger plan and that God had to keep me alive so that this could come to pass!

I also teach the course as a life-changing implementation to those who would like to do what I do by becoming a CARC themselves and carrying the message of love, strength, and hope while helping people recover from trauma and abuse, which often leads to addiction. Not every addiction involves drugs & alcohol. Most addictions start with the delusional thoughts we have, which are also called mental obsessions. "The battlefield is in the mind," – Joyce Meyer. We overcome the mind by changing our thoughts.

We must change everything in order to remain in recovery. We change physically with the cessation of drugs and alcohol and make it a habit to take care of ourselves. We change mentally, healing from the hurt caused by past abuse and traumas. We build toolkits necessary to sustain ourselves mentally and emotionally. We change spiritually, totally surrendering to our Higher Power, knowing He is the only one who can save us, and that in itself is our empowerment. We must sustain and maintain all three of these to avoid the cunning, baffling, insidious disease of the cycle of addiction, and this is a lifelong journey.

I learned that I am only a character in this play called "Life" and do not write the scenes. Everything else is up to the collective in the Kingdom of God. If you love the Lord, all things will work toward your good. As they say, "Keep it simple!"

You may think abstinence is the key to recovery and nothing else. But let me tell you this. Our brains will always follow the path of least resistance. During our addictions, we forged negative pathways in the circuitry of our brains that always had the same result. It wasn't a moral failing – it was not my fault! It was the Cycle of Addiction all over again and again.

Because of years of researching this cycle and studying neurotransmitters and mirror neurons, we formed and changed the circuitry of the brain while in our addiction. Basically, "What wires together, fires together" – Hebb's Law (Donald Hebb, 1949, "The Organization of Behaviors: a Neuropsychological Theory"), which implies we will always find an easier route through the things we are used to doing, even if those actions have negative results, it's still easier to go down that already forged path. Once we abstain from substances and unwanted behavioral patterns, we change our brain's pathways to form new positive pathways. Once we achieve that……repeat, repeat, repeat! **Always do the next right thing! New pathways are formed by new positive behavior repeatedly performed.**

JUST KEEP DOING THE NEXT RIGHT THING

Before you know it, you have performed 100 right things while creating new pathways in the brain. This will change the structure by making it easier to "Do the right thing" through neuroplasticity. You are changing your brain physiologically by forging new pathways; you are (literally) recreating yourself – a whole new you.

Obtaining recovery from any addiction is no easy feat! You will need all of you and your faith, and then you must willingly and knowingly surrender to your Higher Power (God). You must be a willing participant. What makes it so difficult initially is that it is backed by science. The "motivation" neurotransmitter/dopamine is no longer produced naturally by your body. Substances in the body lead to higher-than-normal dopamine production and other neurotransmitters that help your body function correctly (norepinephrine, epinephrine, serotonin, and histamine). These neurotransmitters make you feel good and are meant to be produced naturally. This is (exactly) why you need strength and empowerment outside of yourself. God will do for us what we could not do for ourselves.

Neuroplasticity's change seems daunting, but it isn't; it is the brain's ability to adapt and learn. I think it was designed that way just for a purpose like this. (Basically), we can rewire the brain. Start a new life wherever you are on the scale, and God will bless your life, empowering you to have a paradigm shift and a spiritual experience called a spiritual awakening. One thing is for sure: your life will never be the same.

I know I am valuable to The Kingdom! He did not give up on me: little old me, a country girl from East Tennessee. What I know is that if I weren't, He would have let me die a long time ago! I had a troubled life, and it's not all roses today, but I am free to be me, happy and loved. As I walk this path, I want to be a light shining in a world of darkness. I want to spread hope where there is none, to see smiles where there are only frowns. Seeing folks heal and get past the trauma that caused them so much pain is my ultimate goal.

To be in a place where you feel free to be the person God created you to be, not trying to rely on dissociation to escape – to not only be you....even if it's just for a little while. Numb the hurt, dry the tears, whatever relief you may feel when you are high. Then it all comes crashing down, and you slowly (but surely) lose everything.

The bad part is your mind torments you so much that it is the last thing to go. You are still trying to escape the pain. Jails, institutions, and death - are the results. Which result will people who are addicted experience? We do not know, but I know what the opposite of that is now. I am free from the downward spiral. I am safe, secure, and financially free. I am in the loving arms of my Higher Power, who leads and guides me.

Turn your heartache into blessings. Stop surviving and start thriving! You long for complete love, or you wouldn't have read this. In Him, we get our strength and the courage to change the things we can. Praise God!

I'll be here, working on my dreams and continuing to ***Learn How To Live Because God Would Not Let Me Die!***

Tracy Whitt, CARC

ABOUT THE AUTHOR

TRACY WHITT, CARC

Tracy Whitt, CARC, is a Certified Addiction Recovery Coach who has been very successful in helping others renew their minds and heal the trauma that caused their addictions and unwanted behavioral patterns so that they can maintain their recovery. Tracy currently has the following certifications:

CARC I - Certified Addictions Recovery Coach
CARC II - Certified Abuse Recovery Coach
Spiritual Wellness Coach

She can help anyone interested in these areas: relapse prevention, addiction counseling, unwanted behavioral patterns, abuse/trauma survivors, moving from surviving to thriving, plus many more! She is available for private practice recovery coaching or as a sober companion.
Tracy lives in Nashville, Tennessee/USA, which she calls home since her transformative experience and the making of a whole new life for herself. She enjoys art, old cars, and music when she is not reading or researching topics she loves, such as spirituality, neuroplasticity, how the mind works, and all things to help those in recovery and relapse prevention. She is a true bibliophile at heart.
Her goal is to open a recovery home to help as many people as she can obtain and maintain their recovery.

You may contact her at tracywhitt.carc@gmail.com.

You can learn more about Coach Tracy Whitt by visiting her social media Facebook page here: https://www.facebook.com/profile.php?id=100088345487586.

Website: https://angelonchurchst.com. (Under construction).

CHAPTER SEVEN
FROM VULNERABLE TO VALUABLE
BELINDA OOSTHUIZEN
(SOUTH AFRICA)

INTRODUCTION

Life is a story filled with twists and turns; all that matters is the lessons we learn. Almost everyone has gone through life-changing events at one stage or another. Unconsciously or consciously, we all adapt to change.

My chapter is not only the story of my Voyage through Life; for me, it was a way of escaping my past trauma. I hope it will guide you in staying positive and adapting to an ever-changing life.

Yes, I am stronger than I used to be. But that came at a high price. It cost me more than most people could imagine. It taught me to listen to hope, especially when it tells me there is so much more life to live and more joy and Love to give.

I have learned to let people misunderstand me and gossip about me. What they think of me isn't my problem. Their opinions do not pay my bills; therefore, I will stay kind and committed to Love. I will **NEVER** again let other people make me doubt my worth or the beauty of my worth. Growth will come once you are willing to accept that being lost is part of the process called life and the journey through it.

Life is like a book; some chapters are sad, some are happy, and some are exciting. You will NEVER know what the next chapter has in store if you don't dare to turn the page. With that in mind, I looked at my old life one last time, took a deep breath, and said, "It's time; I'm ready for my new Storybook to begin." Life is not what happens to you; more importantly, how you respond to it that matters.

Remember, you are perfectly imperfect, which makes you perfectly unique. – B.O.O

<u>**THE START OF MY VOYAGE**</u>

At the age of five months, my brother and I were adopted into a loving Christian family. The reason for the adoption was revealed to me after my father's passing in 2019. My adoptive parents had three biological children, and they opened their hearts to my brother and me, who was fourteen months older. Having the blessing of growing up in a house with five boys and two girls was entertaining. My parents didn't smoke, drink, or gamble; they worked very hard. I could not have asked for a better example of Love, kindness, and happiness.

My first bad choice was at the tender age of sixteen when I got involved with a boy who was five years older than me. During my high school years, my parents decided to move to Durban, South Africa (700 km/434.96 miles away). I did not want to move in with them, so I moved in with my then-boyfriend and his family. Alone, unsure, and feeling abandoned, I was thrown into the deep end and had **NO** choice but to swim.

Now alone, unsure, and scared due to the sudden abandonment and new surroundings at a very vulnerable stage in my life, I was thrown into the deep end and had **NO** other choice but to swim.

For the first time in 18 years, I was exposed to gambling & betting on horses, drinking, and drugs. While living with my boyfriend and his family, I got lost and disregarded my safety and goals. Getting high and being drunk, we would go out riding motorbikes, driving at speeds of over 250km/155MPH with no regard for our safety. I was cutting classes to go to the casino and gambling for hours on end.

Being under the legal gambling age in South Africa, I would sit in the car in the parking lot, alone, uncomfortable, and scared. I was trying to concentrate and study for my exams the next day. We would go home after losing thousands of South African Rands (ZAR) in the early mornings, where I had time to sleep for maybe an hour or two and then shower and write my exams. To my complete shock and amazement, I passed.

On the 30th of December 2004, I received my first significant loss. I received a terrible phone call. My brother called with a shaky and sad voice. He told me that my blood-related brother died the night before at the hands of high-jackers. Heartbroken and feeling completely alone, it felt like my whole world was now covered in darkness. I saw my family at the funeral; little did I know I would not see them again for three years. Oh, how life can change in a blink of an eye.

My first job was as a dietician assistant at a well-known Pharmacy in Wonderboom-Suid (South Africa). My life seemed well and on track. I rented a house, and all seemed to be going well. Little did I know that this was the calm before the storm and that my entire world would be flipped upside down!

I am unsure what triggered the change in the man I was with. It started one morning when he got up, took my phone and my bible, locked them in the wall safe, and banned me from contacting any of my friends and family. The following day, I woke up from feeling the pain from a blow to my left cheek. Completely shocked and sleepy, he stood over me and laughed, turned around, and left the house, locking me inside.

He turned the water and lights off and left me with little or no food for days on end while he was gambling away my salary each month. The abuse got worse. He would grab me by my hair and slam me face-first into the doorframe of the room. Most of the time, the blow to my head and face would knock me unconscious. He would bind my hands and feet together with rope/cable ties and place them in a bowl of boiling water while burning me with his cigarettes.

Bruised, bleeding, and in extreme pain, I started crying. He would laugh at me and tell me how pathetic I am. It didn't stop there; he would take clear tape and tape my top eyelids/eyelashes so I couldn't close my eyes completely and forced me to sit through hours of hardcore pornography before sexually abusing me. I was in extreme pain. I felt dirty, used, alone, and scared for my life. But what else was I supposed to do? I was (completely) dependent on him; I had no friends and no contact with my family. I was living my worst nightmare, stuck in a world where I believed this was what I deserved.

I tried to ask for help by opening up to his family about the abuse, only for them to tell me that I was lying. When I showed them the bruises, they would say to me that I deserved it and that I drove him to do it. This abuse and family denial went on for another 12 months. For the first time in my young life, I understood the meaning of being lost, confused, and completely alone. It felt like I was in a world surrounded by monsters and darkness with no way out.

One day, his mother and sister invited us to his mother's house. Once we got there, they decided to go gambling. He locked me in his mother's house and left. I did not know when he would be back, and I was scared for my life. I built up the courage and managed to break the garage door open to get to his mother's office and use her landline to call the only number I could recall, my Dad. With a scared, shaky, soft voice, I told my Dad what happened. He said in a loving and caring tone, "My child, I pray that God will open your eyes and let you see that you are worth more."

It was as if I saw my true self-worth for the first time. My Dad called my brother, who lived in Centurion, and told him where to find me. A short time after I finished talking to my Dad, my brother stopped at the gate to pick me up. I left with only the clothes on my back. I was broken, depressed, extremely thin (at the age of 20, I weighed 35kg/77 pounds), bruised, and my self-esteem was non-existent. I didn't believe that I was worth being treated better.

I resigned from my job; as if the abuse, pain, and anger he took out on me weren't enough, he came in daily to intimidate me and try to take me back home. He followed my brother's car every afternoon to try and find out where I lived. I thought to myself, this is how my life will be. I will always live in constant fear, and this nightmare will NEVER come to an end.

Blessed with two amazing big brothers, they took me in, and a few days later, we visited my Mom & Dad for the first time in many years. When my Dad saw me, he took me into his arms and said: "My child, God brought you back to us, and now you are safe." They sat down with me, and I told them what I had gone through. Everyone just hugged me and showered me with Love. At this very moment, I completely understood the meaning and feeling of true unconditional Love. I was safe!

My first relationship was a colossal failure, and I was a massive failure. I was often asked: "Why did I allow this to happen?" "Why didn't I just up and leave?" The truth is that I was held in captivity, away from my family and their unconditional Love, for such a long time that I believed 110% that this is what Love is. I didn't think I was worth being treated any better! After escaping from this horrific experience, **I thought my nightmare was over. However, I did not realize that what I had been through was one of many failures life had in store for me.**

TRUST IS A HARD LESSON TO LEARN

I thought my nightmare was over. However, I did not realize that what I had been through was one of many failures life had in store for me. The road to recovery was everything but easy, and I was starting my journey. After moving into my brother's house, I began to get my life back on track, or so I thought. The scars left were more profound in my mind, body, and spirit than those visible.

My brother asked me what I would like to do. Remembering what my Dad told me, "Get a degree behind your name! That is the one thing no one will ever be able to take away from you." I decided to study even though it wasn't my passion and was not on my list of career fields. From my tests, it was, however, something to keep my mind occupied and get me into a new circle of friends. While studying, I met some fantastic individuals, and some are still part of my life today.

They took me out one night to a concert. I was fragile, self-conscious, and extremely shy. I was standing in the crowd, not really having fun, just keeping to myself, when suddenly, some random guy placed his hand on my shoulder, looked me straight in the eye, and said with a very calm, friendly tone of voice, "Relax, smile and enjoy the evening, beautiful."

Completely shocked and disgusted, I asked, "Who does he think he is? He does not know me." My brother laughed, smiled, and said, "Not all men are bad! You see what happens when you go out by yourself." I realized I needed to learn to trust others again, relax, and have fun. I did not know that I needed to learn to identify those who would respect me and guide me with false smiles and masks of trust.

In 2007, my second year of studies, my brother bought a house in Hartebeespoort Dam (An area near Brits in Gauteng, South Africa) and moved out. My oldest brother left every Friday afternoon to stay with my other brother in the guest house as it was closer to the golf course, meaning I was alone on Friday nights until late Saturday afternoons.

I took full advantage of my new freedom and went out almost every Friday night. I decided one night to join my friend and go to a nearby club with her boyfriend and his friend. As a rule, we never went out alone; we always went in pairs. **Going out with my girlfriend was where I had my first lesson on who to trust and who not to trust.**

We entered the club just after 20:00 hours (8 pm). It was Friday night, and we knew most of the students there. I didn't drink any alcohol. I asked for coke with ice every time. Around 24:30/11:30 pm, I noticed the room spinning and felt sick. We left the club, drifting in and out of consciousness. I noticed we weren't driving on the road to my brother's flat. Scared and confused, I thought to myself at least my friend would look after me.

I remember the car stopping at an unfamiliar house, being helped out of the car, and placed on a bed as I continued drifting in and out of consciousness. All I remember was the blurred faces of her boyfriend and his friend. My body was forceable moving, and I could feel the pain as they took turns raping me. I passed out and woke up the next morning, still confused, bruised, and in extreme pain. I realized that I had no idea where I was.

I carefully walked out of the room and saw my friend standing there. I asked her where we were and if she could remember anything from when we left the club last night. She smiled at me and said in a low tone, calm voice, she did not. I saw her boyfriend and, in a frail and concerned tone of voice, asked them to take me home. I used the "My brother will expect me home in 30 minutes card," and they took me home. I was ashamed, confused, scared, and felt dirty. I sat next to my friend in the backseat, not saying a word the entire ride home.

As they stopped to drop me off, I exited the car and went through security to my brother's flat as fast as my two skinny legs could carry me. Knowing he would not be home before 1500/3 pm. I immediately got into the shower, and it was there that it hit me like a brick wall. I was drugged and raped. I sat in the shower, fully dressed, while the water was still running, crying my eyes out and asking myself how this happened. Did I not learn anything?

Sitting there, all I could think of was that I was a failure again. I failed to learn from my past mistakes and allowed myself to be taken advantage of again. This time around, I got angry! How can men be like that? How can men treat women with little to no regard and do with them as they please?

I felt used and broken all over again. I started being distant and quiet and kept to myself. I began isolating myself, didn't go out, and did not want to be alive anymore. I didn't tell a single soul about the events of that night. If I keep it to myself, I believe it will be as if it **NEVER** happened. I can't admit to yet another defeat and failure. **Life knocked me down yet again.**

WHAT GOES UP MUST COME DOWN

For the remainder of my second year, I focused on my studies. My circle of friends was extremely small. My nights out were mostly with my brother or my best friends, consisting of four people. I never went out without one of them by my side and made sure that if we went somewhere, we drove our (own) vehicle, and if I didn't know you, I didn't have time for you.

I calmed down in my third and final year of studies. I started working part-time to get independent and keep myself occupied over weekends. I graduated in January 2009. For the first time in years, my life was calm and boring. I successfully kept the events of that night locked away in my subconscious mind.

I started working at a well-known company in February 2009. For the first time since 2004, life seemed to turn a positive corner for me. I was extremely good at sales. I won the Top Dealership Sales Advisor Award in July and the Dealership Department Top Advisor Award in 2009. A new group of friends surrounded me, and the past seemed to have been forgotten.

As impossible as it seemed, I met someone, fell in love, married, and had a beautiful baby girl in July 2010. I had a reason to succeed, be happy, and live for. The relationship wasn't smooth sailing. We had our ups and downs and our fights, but compared to my past and the relationship six years ago, I was happy and content with where my life was heading.

I won more awards as the years went by. I was included in the Top Conversation Ratio 130% January 2013, Top Advisor February 2013, Most Improved Salary February 2013, Top Conversion Advisor 86,84% February 2013, to name a few. My life was back on track. I was successful and could not be happier.

I was headhunted by another company and decided to take the opportunity, and I resigned in July 2013. A decision I would end up regretting. The new company was an hour's drive from where we stayed, and I had to drive through dangerous areas. After the third hijacking attempt, I decided to resign. I had a toddler who needed her mother, and I couldn't gamble with my life.

I went to an interview and spoke to the manager, who advised me that I would receive the job offer in the morning and that my start date would be the 2nd week of January 2014. Sad to say, that never happened. When I decided to go to their head office to inquire, I was informed that the vacancy had been filled internally and that the new manager had started in December 2013. I was angry, scared, and confused. What now? Where do I go from here?

It was 05:00 am, and I was dressed professionally with nowhere to go. For the first time in many years, my daily routine was interrupted. While sitting at the desk going through hundreds of job advertisements, I got an unexpected call from my husband. Panicked, he said: "Hide all the external hard drives." Fifteen minutes later, he opens the door with two investigators from his company.

They demanded to come into the house. My reaction was calm and collective, yet very confused. I took out my phone and called my lawyer. I placed the call on the speaker and advised him on what the situation was. My lawyer informed them that they were not allowed to enter my private residential house without a court order, and if they did not remove themselves from the premises, he would contact the police.

The investigators left along with my husband. An hour later, my husband walked in, box in hand. He looked at me and said, "I messed up." I looked at him and said, "Do not tell me any more detail. The less I know, the better". The following day, I received a call from his company, and they told me what was going on. My husband allegedly decided to take some client details from their company and share them with an employee I worked for. I advised them that they were more than welcome to look at all my emails, listen to all my phone calls, and look at my cell phone data. I had nothing to do with it and had nothing to hide.

They could not find any evidence and thanked me for cooperating. However, I was found guilty by association just because we were married. They advised me that I would never be able to work for them again. I was shocked and angry, and I felt defeated.

It broke my trust in my husband. Not only did he manage to blacklist himself, but he damaged my reputation and future in the industry. I could not look at him the same way. I filed for divorce and told him to move out. I was devastated and broken as I failed again. This time, my failure was much more significant; I failed myself and my daughter. **The higher you climb up, the harder you hit the ground when you fall.**

HITTING ROCK BOTTOM

One Friday morning, I picked up the newspaper and found an ad for sales managers with a decent monthly salary. I decided it was faith, and I would email them a complete list of my academic credentials in my CV/Curriculum vitae. At 1500/3:00 pm that afternoon, I received a phone call, and they asked me to come in on Monday morning for an interview. There was light at the end of the tunnel.

I felt good Saturday and Sunday about receiving the call. When Monday morning rolled around, I got up, dressed, and went for my interview, thinking very optimistic. When I arrived, I was notified that I was one of thirty people invited for this interview. We all were asked to enter the room. As we sat there, a young, well-dressed man introduced himself and said everyone had a questionnaire to complete in 15 minutes. After receiving the questionnaire results, he called us into his office two at a time. I was successful and given my toolkit and file. I was instructed to be at the office at 08:00 am the following day to sign my contract. I went home extremely positive and hopeful.

The job was demanding, with extended hours, and I was emotionally and physically drained. I was about to give up and resign when I was informed that we would be leaving on a business trip for two weeks. This vacation was just what I needed to get away and place my focus on my work. I discussed the necessary arrangements with my daughter and packed my bags. Within those two weeks, I managed to turn my luck around; I got promoted to senior consultant.

In March, I received a promotion to sales manager, and I was informed that we would be leaving on a business trip to the Northern Cape in two days. I was excited and optimistic. I needed to complete my last leg to be promoted to Junior Director and start my own branch. Little did I know what life had planned for me next.

The group of twelve consisted of one Director, two Sales Managers, three Senior Sales Consultants, and six Junior Sales Consultants, for a total of four women and eight men. We took three vehicles to transport all twelve team members. We reached our destination and started setting up the tents. The Director advised everyone to cool down in the pool, and then we would sit down for dinner.

I got up at 06:00 am to shower. As I showered, I heard someone entering the ladies' restroom. I thought nothing of it until I heard them locking the gate. I thought, "Don't stress; you have a key." The next moment, the Director opened the shower curtain, got in, and forced himself on me. I was scared and determined, but I tried to fight him off. I was not strong enough, and he raped me. Afterward, he got out, dressed, and said: "You are mine now, do you understand?"

I did not know what to do. I did not believe what had happened. I was in complete shock, discussed, and in pain. I sat down in the corner of the shower for what felt like hours. I got enough strength and courage to get up and dressed. I dried my hair, put my make-up on, practiced smiling as if nothing was wrong, and went to our campsite to join the rest of the group, who were completely unaware of what just happened to me.

One of the senior sales consultants noticed that I was acting strangely. I told her what happened, and she got up and confronted the Director. He told her I was lying and that it never happened, and she believed him. I was 1700km/1056.331 miles) away from home, and I knew it was my word against his. I decided not to think of it and place my focus on my work.

After that morning, I made sure not to go alone to the bathroom and always had a female junior consultant with me while working. This way, it will prevent him from getting me alone. I made sure not to pull any attention to myself and focus on my work.

On the last day of our two-week business trip, after all deliveries were completed, we had to decide if we would stay over one more night or drive back home. One of our clients warned us not to drive at night due to the farm animals in the area. Out of the twelve, five of us, including myself, voted to stay the night and leave the following day. We were outvoted by seven who wanted to go.

The Director told us we had to pay for our accommodation and petrol/gas if we wanted to stay. Remember, we have not been paid for our sales, and none of us could afford it.

We advised the Director of this, and he looked at us and said: "I am the Director, and if I say we leave tonight, we leave." He grabbed my car keys out of my hand and got behind the steering wheel; looking at me, he said, "Get in, or stay and find your (own) way home." I looked at him and said, "This is my car." He laughed, saying, "Either you get in, or I will leave you here." I had no choice, so I got into the passenger side of my car. One of the junior consultants, Herman, got into the back seat, and we left.

We stopped at a garage to get some food and drinks and got back on the road. At about 23:00 hrs/11:00 pm, we reached the halfway point (406 kilometers/252 miles from Upington) between Vryburg and Kuruman (North West Province, South Africa). As we drove around the curve, a herd of thirteen cows slowly crossed the road about fifty meters/164 feet ahead of us. For those who don't know, a cow's eyes do not reflect when a light is shined on it. With nowhere to go and our driving speed was about 110km/68 miles per hour, we knew we were in trouble.

It felt like everything was moving in slow motion. All I can recall from the accident itself was the consultant in the back screaming out a swear word, the Director pushing my legs down (I was sitting with my feet on the dashboard), and the brakes screaming. It was quiet for a little while. I began to feel relieved as I thought to myself, we stopped in time, and then it started raining cows, literally speaking! Cows were crossing the road just as our car went out of control. While crossing the road, one cow hit the right front side of my car, causing it to flip over and land on the roof. Another cow flipped onto the bonnet/hood of the car, and I was ready to make peace with the fact that it would land on my lap.

The car was spinning for what felt like an eternity. Finally, we came to a complete stop with the nose of the car pointing towards the direction we came from. I hit my head against the side window and remember seeing a cow's head on the other side hitting the window at the same time. None of the six airbags deployed, but we were alive.

The other team members pulled over and immediately pushed the car off the road. I do not know how we managed to get out of the vehicle as both front doors could only open about 15 cm/5.19 inches or so. The Director got out and asked if we were okay. I got out, rattled, confused, cold, and in shock. I sat down on the side of the road and called my insurance company to report what happened and where we were.

My brother told me I called him about the accident and asked him to tell my Mom and Dad the following day. I can't remember this at all. I was told that around 00:30/12:30 am, the police arrived at the accident scene, took statements, and advised us that the tow truck had arrived. I was standing next to the tow truck when one of the junior consultants told me that my ankles were swollen and blood or something was coming out of my left ear.

We waited to see if an ambulance would arrive, but it never did. I went to sit in the 4x4 pickup truck of the other senior sales consultant and lost consciousness, and I blacked out. What happened next, I was told by my colleague. They drove to the nearest hospital. When they arrived, they walked into what seemed to be a scene out of a horror movie. The lights were flickering on and off. There was not a living soul in sight, bloody clothes on the floor, and the smell of death was in the air. They turned around and went back to the car. They drove for about 50km/31 miles to the nearest 24-hour clinic, where I was treated and sent home.

LIST OF SOME OF MY INJURIES FROM THE CAR ACCIDENT:

- Soft tissue injury – cervical spine.
- Soft tissue injury – lumbar spine.
- Torn ligaments – both ankles.
- Base of skull fracture involving the left middle cranial fossa.
- Panic Disorder with agoraphobia.
- Major Depressive Disorder.
- Post Traumatic Stress Syndrome (PTSD).
- 35% hearing loss in my left ear.
- Chronic cervicogenic headaches.

I was informed that the company lawyer would handle our claims and book appointments with their doctors. I was sent home to rest. We arrived at the office Monday morning only to find the building empty and no soul in sight. I asked my colleague to drive to the Directors' house to find out what was happening. We arrived at his residential house only to see it was empty. They were gone, and we have not received our salaries? Confused, in pain and shock, we looked at each other, and all we could say was, "What now? **We have hit Rock Bottom!**

ROAD TO RECOVERY

I have been unemployed since May 2014, not because of the difficulty finding employment and endlessly applying for jobs. I received numerous interview requests for sales positions but had to leave empty-handed because I had no reliable transport/vehicle. Remember, my car was a total loss from the accident, and I could not afford to replace it. I was asked to leave my flat because I could not pay my rent. I was behind on all my payments, and my credit score was lowered to the red zone. I did not qualify for any loans; I could not get financing for a vehicle. That accident left my life in ruins.

In November 2014, I received a phone call from a well-known (JSE) Johannesburg Stock Exchange-listed recruitment company, which allowed me to start earning an income again. As the training began, I was told I would never succeed in the industry. After making numerous successful placements and invoicing over R1.5 million (Rand)/$80,833, I left the company and moved to Cape Town.

I was unemployed from April 2015 until November 2015. I started (working) as the Executive Marketing and Recruitment Manager at a Wynberg recruitment agency. I assisted in getting this small business up and running on the same systems as my previous company. I empowered the three junior recruiters with the needed training and managed to invoice over R580 000/$31.255.51 in four months. Sadly, due to my success, the directors changed the commission structure and payout without following the correct procedures. I pointed this out to management. To my surprise, due to financial difficulties, the company had no other choice but to let me go. At least, that's what the company told me. At 29 years old, I got retrenched/removed from my job.

Lost, confused, and filled with negative thoughts, I got up one morning and decided to attend a seminar with a well-known motivational speaker and business coach. It was a long day, and I wasn't very optimistic about what they told us. I told myself it was just a money-making scheme and wanted to leave the seminar on three (separate) occasions.

But I don't particularly appreciate starting something and not finishing it. I was brought up in a way that taught me it would be disrespectful to leave before the end. So I stayed, and it was one of my best decisions ever. I made the right decision and invested in their #1 Signature program and book. I am positive, determined, and ready to start my own recruitment company and make it a success. I joined their Business Coaching Club and started surrounding myself with some of the world's most successful business owners. I followed the instructions and learned by observing what they do and how they run their companies.

Through their program, I met amazing people worldwide. I dedicated myself to the program and was exposed to the fascinating business world as part of the team. They assisted me with my company. I partnered with people from the UK, Chicago, Dubai, New Zealand, and Sweden. I followed their advice and guidance and grew a successful international recruitment agency.

After everything I have been through, all the storms, waves of trouble, wrong decisions, choices, and hard knocks of failures, I kept on going, never losing faith, never giving up, and trusting in the knowledge, dedication, and self-belief that empowered me to be successful. (All because) **I invested in a business coach and started changing how I perceived my situation. When you change the way you look at things, the things you look at change.**

HOW DID I DO THAT?

The lessons I took from my short voyage thus far and the challenges that came with them have empowered me never to lose hope and keep faith in a brighter tomorrow. It wasn't easy; it was an internal battle I had to endure. It was challenging to get out of the negative frame of mind. I needed to understand that sometimes you must burn bridges and cut ties with certain people to reach your visions, goals, and dreams.

I needed to understand that the front window of my vehicle was bigger than the rear-view window for a reason. The same is true in life! It's not where I came from and what I've been through; it's how I dealt with my many unforeseen bumps in the road, obstacles, defeats, failures, and setbacks that matter most. I needed to let go of my past and focus on the future. If I hadn't gone through this voyage in life, I would not be the person I am today. Today, I wake up each morning happy to face a new day, open to accepting and noticing the small blessings all around me. I tackle any problem head-on and always find the solution.

Do I still fail? Yes, of course I do. However, I learned from my mistakes and walked away from them, taking only the lesson learned. As the caterpillar struggled before transforming into a beautiful butterfly, I changed. You can change your situation and turn your excuses and fears into motivation and drive. You must control how you think, feel, and act when faced with adversity.

ABOUT THE AUTHOR

BELINDA OOSTHUIZEN

- ✓ **See your failures as a beginning, not an end.** If you fail at something, ask yourself: "What can I do differently the next time so I don't fail again?
- ✓ **Make peace with the past and leave it there.** Don't drag your past behind you like a chair you want to sit on when life knocks you down again.
- ✓ **Turn your mistakes into lessons.** Mistakes are there to tell us we have done something wrong.
- ✓ **You and only you can determine your self-worth.** Put boundaries and standards in place and keep to them. If someone does not meet these standards, they are not the right person for you. Become your (own) gatekeeper!
- ✓ **Change the way you perceive your situation.** Once you make the mental choice to change the way you see your situation, taking action to change it will drive you. Instead of asking, "Why me? "Stand back and say "Why not me?"
- ✓ **Assume nothing and question everything.** If you don't understand something, ask questions until you do.
- ✓ **Believe in yourself and your abilities.** Self-confidence can only start from within; it is not something someone else can give you.
- ✓ **Invest in an excellent coach.** An excellent Coach will be there with you all the way to celebrate every success and empower you from every mistake.
- ✓ **Don't be afraid to cut ties and burn bridges with those who don't bring value to your life.** Surround yourself with people you can learn from and know will be there for you through good and bad times.
- ✓ **Never lose hope, and keep standing strong in your faith.** Faith and hope are like a WIFI signal; you can't see it, but you can believe and trust it is there.

I want to thank my dear friend and brother, Coach Michael Bart Mathews, "The Gentle Giant," for seeing me as a winner, achiever, and not just a survivor but an empowering thriver. Big Mike and Robbie, thank you both for believing in me.

My dear readers, if I can do it, so can you!
STOP making excuses because any excuse is a reason to fail.

Belinda Oosthuizen

CHAPTER EIGHT
ROAD TO RECOVERY
THE RUNNING GIRL
LAMIS CHKEIR (LEBANON)

As a child, Lamis thinks of herself as the queen of running, always running to find a sense of belonging. She feels as distant as the stars among the people she loves the most. No matter what she encounters, she feels alone, and on her tiny shoulders, Lamis carries the heavy weight of solitude and displacement from each of the six houses she has moved from in less than two years.

With so many moves comes the ache of feeling like an immigrant in her own country, which drives her to search for a place to call "home." As an adolescent, she feels like an outsider in her (own) house, primarily due to her parents building thick walls of noncommunication between rooms to avoid warmth and affection. Lamis keeps a silent record of all the unspoken expectations and unkept promises. Lamis, feeling the need to escape, follows her like shadows on the wall. She will run away from this to heal her bleeding heart.

As a young woman, Lamis escapes to crowded cities, experiencing different vibrant energies, yet still followed by the shadows from her childhood. And so, while engaged in her work, among her close circle of friends, and while carrying out her family responsibilities, she meets many people. While peering deep into the black holes of their eyes, searching for a savior, she finds herself adrift in a sea of darkness and unfulfilled longing. She finds nothing.

For those passing through her life, Lamis gives them what they need, knowing that they won't stay long or provide anything in return. Disappointment becomes another shadow – one that escapes the wall to suffocate her with a tight grip.

Rather than being an active participant, Lamis is a silent observer who questions everything, even the simple smile of another. But she is also a fighter, and whenever she feels like giving up, a feeling of hope rises again from believing in the possibility of getting what she wants. As a thinker, the only truth she faces is the certainty of death.

As a young girl born into a socioeconomic and cultural system of contradictions, Lamis's family experience helped her understand the big picture of Lebanese society. Her extended family was a great example of where all contradictions coexisted- feudalism, racism, ethnic and religious discrimination, ignorance, conservatism, and liberalism, to name a few.

Lamis's grandfather, a dashing lieutenant in the French army during the Mandate and from a wealthy family from Byblos, met her grandmother, a humble farmer who captured his heart. He was a great gambler, eventually losing most of his fortune. Stories of his adventures never ended. Lamis didn't know much about her mother's lineage, but when she asked, the only answer she got was that they were from another province in the south and had decided to come to Bekaa (Lebanon), where they changed their last name.

Because of the war, her father's family moved to Bekaa (Lebanon), where her father met her mother. Lamis was born the youngest of four in a small village, where she formed a deep bond with her grandmother and aunt, who helped raise her.

One day, when she was four, Lamis ran next door. Her heart pounded like a drum as she darted up the narrow stairs. Behind her, she could hear the heavy footsteps of her angry father. She pushed herself, ran faster, and jumped into her grandmother's bed. She held her breath, once again escaping from the violence as she often did to a place where she could finally breathe in this beautiful world of imagination. With difficulty, her grandmother told her stories because the stroke she suffered after hearing the news of her youngest son's death in the Lebanese civil war paralyzed half her body and face. When her angry son enters her room, she yells at him to go home!

Lamis is safe. Grandma starts to tell her a story:

Once upon a time, a little girl lived in a faraway village. Whenever she wanted to go somewhere, she used her magical wool ball. Placing the ball on the ground, it magically started moving toward the destination, and the girl would follow. One day, as she ventured out to fetch her grandmother's necessities, the ball suddenly stopped on her journey back, leaving the little girl stranded in an unfamiliar, desolate street far from home. Fear and frustration gripped her tiny body. Her attempts to make it work failed. Alone, she stood in the middle of the fading sunlight, tears streaming down her cheeks. With each passing moment, the darkness descended until she found herself trapped in the darkness, with no magical wool ball to lead her home and no one in sight to offer assistance.

This was the first but not the only time Lamis recalled when she and her siblings, along with their cousins, used to gather to hear a new story before they went back to their homes. The tradition of her grandma's storytelling became a cherished part of Lamis's routine to escape her parents' fights, which is why she wished they would've just divorced.

Back at home one day, with her dark brown eyes filled with tears and her face filled with bruises, she looked angrily at her mom, who convinced her father to accept a new job offer, which meant uprooting them from their familiar surroundings yet again. She knew that her mother aimed to escape her husband's family, all while under the pretext of their new economic situation caused by the war, where luxuries became a distant dream.

Living with a working mother wasn't easy for five siblings. Lamis helped her mother with the kitchen duties. She could never forget some things, like when her mother offered delicious sweets to their weekly visitors. Lamis could recall the loud voices and laughter as her mother greeted them with repeated "Welcome! Welcome!" Until one day, a bomb exploded just outside the kitchen window, with Lamis close by. Lebanon was caught in the midst of chaos from a civil war, and as a young girl, Lamis found herself trying to escape from the dangers outside the house, only to have to face those dangers inside the house as well.

From the car window, squeezed in with her siblings, Lamis said goodbye to her little memories of her current house. While on their way to the new destination, everywhere they drove at that time was followed by the same disheartening scene. A Syrian soldier halts their car, demanding her father's identity in a humiliating and aggressive manner, before reluctantly allowing them to pass.

After many checkpoints, they arrived, but all they found was a small room that upset her father so much that he immediately started the search for a new place. Finally, they settled in a house in the middle of a field, in the middle of nowhere, where the closest neighbor was at least a mile away.

At their new school, Lamis and her sister, along with their mother and all women and girls, were asked to wear a hijab to reflect the values and beliefs of the institution's founder. For her mother, it was only a dress code, a simple work requirement of being a French teacher. However, for Lamis, it was a new kind of imprisonment that she could not escape, suffocating her from the first day. As a reaction to her new look, Lamis no longer attended family events, not even her uncle's wedding. It was her way of running away from any social gathering.

Because of this, additional conflict arose inside the family. Her mother dared not stand up to this decision since it was her duty, but her aunt went crazy knowing they had to follow these strict rules. Listening to Lamis's mother and Aunty fight, the young girls were divided into two camps- one which (totally) rejected this new habit. And the other who considered it forbidden not to follow. Lamis's tiny brain couldn't understand why this was happening and why her brothers got to go to another school for a better education while she and her sister had to stay in this backward place. While her mother's decision may have been influenced by the necessity of maintaining their employment at the school rather than their conviction of its actual importance, the truth was that Lamis' father liked the idea, believing that the hijab would offer protection and help guide his daughters on the right path. But despite his best efforts to convince her, it did not.

For Lamis, memorizing and applying the Ten Commandments in her daily life was easier and more enjoyable. She was a true believer by nature, and overall, her parents' effort in raising the family with strong morals and ethics kept her well-behaved, especially when she said a bad word. Using profanity or curse words was a red line they could never cross.

Being a math teacher, solving problems was built into her father's character. He was a traditional man with his (own) sense of perceived injustice. Always upset, he dedicated himself to his work, trying to ensure a better life for his three sons. Like any stereotypical patriarch, he was worried about his daughters as females in a masculine society. He focused on raising his daughters to be obedient wives who would uphold his honor. In gatherings with his friends, he would famously joke that "**Having three sons was a blessing until 'this' came and broke the lineage,**" an obvious hint at his preference for boys.

Lamis's full lips remained sealed shut in fear of objecting. No one dared say a word. Even her oldest teenage brother could not ask 'why.' It didn't matter because she knew the answer: "Shut your ugly mouth!" Lamis's reaction was to hide her thoughts and the words that came out of her mouth so as not to trigger her mother. Mental and physical bullying was sadly tolerated. Lamis's self-esteem decreased, and any sense of belonging had nearly disappeared, leading her to blame herself for even living. This was the first time she considered escaping life itself.

To run from all this, Lamis would walk on sunny days alone near her place, tears flowing down her plump cheeks and the breeze caressing her dark hair. With every step, the feeling of running would increase! Maybe she wished for a magical intervention to offer her passage to a destiny away from her reality. But as the sun was about to set each time, she gave up, for there was no magic wool ball to guide her, and all she could do was go back. Nobody even noticed her return or her absence. But where else could Lamis run? Her grandparents' home was now too far, and it was time for her monthly visit, so she had to stay and endure.

Life became harder, with the financial crisis escalating more and more in Lebanon, and Lamis's family, just like thousands of others, found themselves in a struggle for survival, which affected everyone's mental health. The war managed to kill everything in them, even hope. The entire family had to support their father planting and harvesting his vast lands. Lamis enjoyed working with her father, especially when they made a game of who could harvest the most. She preferred this to being inside, cleaning the house, where even as a young child, she bore the heavy weight of responsibility on her tiny shoulders. She worked harder and harder, always trying to earn her parents' attention, appreciation, or love. But instead, it was her brother and sister in her parent's arms, and this was torture for Lamis.

The scent of new clothes became a distant memory. The sight of toys to play with, no playgrounds during the holidays, and no friends or cousins to share happy moments with became a distant memory. Instead, Lamis and her sister enjoyed simple activities, like trying to repair their broken plastic dolls' missing limbs or matted hair.

Nature became her most trustworthy friend. As the first rays of sunlight awakened Lamis each day, a symphony of nature greeted her sounds: the ducks with their soft quacks and splashing applauding her, the regal rooster proudly announcing the welcome of day, the goose and her fluffy chicks chirping to remind her how beautiful she was-these were her only friends. She kept herself busy with her new companions on her father's mini farm located in the backyard. Hunting for eggs was her favorite pastime, a game of hide and seek, and she discovered hidden treasures with her tiny, gentle hands.

One day, amidst the crowded funeral for their landlord, Lamis escaped the overwhelming procession of mourning guests to her favorite place in the backyard. Seeking solace and lost in her thoughts, Lamis didn't notice the boy until he almost sat beside her. She was surprised when he reached out his hand to touch her. Lamis couldn't understand what he wanted, but her intuition told her this was wrong. He asked her if she wanted to play "House" with him. So, with a quick reflective response, she answered, "Let's play; catch me if you can!" Lamis ran as quickly as she could, passing straight through the funeral to the attic, where she used to hide and pass her time. Running was her favorite sport, but little did she know how many times she would have to use it to protect herself, like when she had to run from two men trying to kidnap her just a few months afterward. That was a traumatic memory.

Many storms hit the little girl's world at the same time. At home, her observant eyes witnessed the harsh realities of life so early, when she used to have to listen to her parents' friend's problems when they visited, which exposed her to things beyond her age. Even at school, it was normal for students to get abused. Hitting was something normal at that time. Chaos outside and turmoil inside raged within her. Lamis grew more and more aggressive and was given the new nickname **"stubborn girl."**

The idea of God's nature confused her: between being merciful and loving or just and fair. Sometimes, Lamis liked the idea of punishment to satisfy her need for justice against those who hurt her and others. Like any child exposed to a different religion than how they were raised, Lamis' first questions about the concept of God, his nature, and his dwelling made her curious but also lost. She found comfort in listening to the myriad of stories about God – from Satan's fall to creation. To Adam and Eve, the angels, ancient kings, prophets, and their miracles, to Jesus and Mary. All these stories enriched her imagination in such a way that she was always trying to find a common point among them all.

One day, fed up with the isolated 'Open-air prison' and the conditions they lived in, Lamis and her siblings organized a peaceful protest with a dozen taped papers on all the walls of the house and main doors stating their demands. Accompanied by her siblings, Lamis beat plastic pots like drums and chanted loudly, "We want to go back!" Their parents agreed because they were disappointed with their situation and moved back to their first house, closest to their relatives and civilization. However, the once-beloved dream home was not the same. Grandma had passed away, taking all its charm with her. The only person Lamis had left was her Auntie.

Removing the hijab was the next thing Lamis did to push back against the rules. Her father objected and tried to stop her, but eventually came to understand that she was not a little girl anymore who could so easily be controlled. Everything had a price, and this time, it meant no more support (at all), not even her pocket money. But to Lamis, it was the price of freedom, so it was worth it.

One afternoon, while watching her father giving a student a private lesson, Lamis offered to help when she saw that he was losing control over his temper with the stubborn boy. Her father relinquished the student to her, and more students were to follow. Day after day, Lamis succeeded in this, her first "Real" job working from home, which served her well since she later had her own three kids to help with their homework.

"Stranger" was her new nickname in that old familiar place. As Lamis got older, she realized that the village was made up of families based on their last names. A tradition that made them all proud of family lineages. Anyone from outside was considered a " stranger." When she later broke up with her first boyfriend because of this kind of prejudice, Lamis started to understand what her parents themselves had experienced and had tried to protect them from. As someone who came to defend human rights, she found the concept of discrimination based on family ties incomprehensible.

Her three brothers traveled to pursue their studies outside the country, and Lamis and her sister now found themselves alone with their parents in Beirut, a cosmopolitan city. Her father gave her no option but to enroll in a public university with almost negligible tuition fees. Instead, she chose to work hard to get a private university education, which wasn't too hard for Lamis despite being a pressing challenge.

At that time, good grades alone couldn't secure a good scholarship. Lamis had to find a full-time job. After working all day, she would head to college, often staying until 9 pm. Her sister helped support her by not only accepting to go to the public university to save them some money but also by working while she was studying and giving Lamis money along the way.

These efforts enabled her to finance her education and helped shape her. It was during a work event that Lamis met her second boyfriend. Yet, she soon understood that religious differences were another obstacle for him and his family. This time, religious prejudice broke up her relationship. It was just another way Lamis started to see how the war had poisoned the minds and souls of people in her society.

Stepping back from such complexities, she focused on her career and found a way to work and live outside the country. All she wanted was to be away from this toxic society. Lamis finally realized she was a stranger in her own country, not just in that village. However, traveling alone wasn't acceptable to her parents, and even though she had gained financial independence, she didn't have the total freedom to live alone. She understood the only way was to find a partner willing to live abroad. She eventually met a guy who welcomed the idea. After all this, hope was risen again. Surprisingly, he fell in love with her, and she was open and honest with him.

From the beginning, Lamis told him about her plans, and when love was the only language he spoke, he supported her. Months after they met, in 2006, Lebanon was engulfed in the chaos of the July War. Due to Beirut's small geographic size, relocating to a safer area became necessary, as the impact of the strikes felt uncomfortably close. Again, where was there to run? Lamis was not married or engaged. Cohabitation wasn't an option for both conservative families, and so they had to wait.

Two years later, she was married at the age of twenty-four. The wedding ceremony announced freedom, more than a big party. After the marriage, it was time to begin work on the immigration papers. They passed through obstacles in the months ahead until she had her first son. Having a family was something almost sacred to her. Lamis dropped her work in TV production to take care of her son. She poured all the love she wished for herself into her new small family, willing to do whatever it took to build and protect it.

During her first pregnancy, Lamis discovered that she had extremely low blood platelets, so the doctor advised her to stop the pregnancy. Lamis decided to get pregnant again; regardless of the consequences, she was intent on giving her son a brother or sister. Already sensing that her marriage may not survive in the future, she was determined to give her older child a sibling just in case Lamis did not survive its birth; they would at least have each other.

Life took another direction. She got pregnant again, and in the 5th month, from the ultrasound, her doctor claimed that there was a high percentage that her baby girl had a high rate of Down

Syndrome symptoms, and abortion was his advice. Lamis (strongly) refused the idea and did not allow anyone to interfere with her decision, not even her husband and his family. Since abortion wasn't an option for her, she also refused to do the amnio test because of its consequences – due to the risk of harming the baby. For the first time in her life, Lamis agreed with her parents. Since she had gotten married, their relationship progressed nicely. There was nothing to fear because now she was carrying another man's name.

Refusing everyone's interference, Lamis stayed home, talking to nobody, until she reached delivery time. Her main problem still existed. The possibility of a normal delivery was almost zero; a c-section was the only choice, even though it was a considerable risk to her life. For that reason, she had to stay one month in the hospital for blood treatment, which failed. Left with no other options, they had to operate. If they had waited any longer, even just one day, Lamis and the baby would not have survived.

The worst decision was to do the operation without full anesthesia. Lamis spent many long, hard nights thinking about her little boy being alone if she died. But God intervened, and one day before her operation, and with no medical explanation, the platelet count went back up, so the risk of bleeding was lower. Lamis was fully awake. Although she had local anesthesia, she still felt every cut and every stitch. After giving birth, Lamis was blessed with a beautiful, healthy baby girl. She felt incredibly grateful to her Lord, who finally answered all her prayers.

Three weeks later, Lamis woke up at 3 am to check on her baby girl. She screamed because her baby girl's face was as dark as the night. Lamis could tell that her baby girl was not breathing. Within minutes, her husband took them to the hospital. All the way, Lamis held her baby girl, crying and praying, asking God to intervene again. They arrived at the emergency room, where they immediately put the baby on oxygen, and after weeks in intensive care, the danger was finally over. Sitting next to her tiny angel, holding her hand, which was tired from all the IV pricks, Lamis looked at her brilliant eyes and felt the urge to write her daughter's first poem.

Finally, they went back home. Lamis used to hear about how health was such a great blessing but never understood it as well as she did after all of that traumatic experience. That year was challenging but full of lessons that helped her appreciate God's gift of health to each person.

The first three years of marriage weren't easy, but they endured hard times together. Initially, their story blossomed until problems started seeping into their marriage. Lamis (first) faced her husband's negligence of her feelings and lack of communication. She sensed that something had changed. He started hiding important information, even their first immigration document she'd been long waiting for. Maybe he enjoyed his job so much that he didn't want to leave it. Or perhaps he discovered they weren't a good match and only they found an escape through each other. Or maybe having an additional responsibility was too heavy to support. It seemed he couldn't understand why Lamis insisted on living abroad, this **"running girl,"** as he used to call her. Maybe they both misunderstood that marriage was supposed to be a mutual union where healing and growth occurred, and together, they would be better for each other. There was no fairytale ending for Lamis and her husband. Their marriage would end in due time.

Years passed, and with the help of her mother and sister, Lamis managed to continue her work projects in many different countries. Taking different projects, the runner found a temporary escape to the nearby Arab countries, Europe, the US, and Africa. She didn't miss any chance to take a potential project abroad. She enjoyed adventures and discovery as she was exposed to different cultures and beautiful people. These projects did not only maintain her financial needs but also gave her a profound understanding of people's differences. When shooting, her weekly visits to Lebanon were only to see her kids. Nobody else knew about her comings and goings. She managed most of her work online to have time with her family. Being in the communication field helped her maintain this equilibrium between her family and her work. Still, it also affected her marriage, with each one growing in their separate directions until they finally agreed to divorce.

Lamis began to clearly understand that the problem wasn't just with her wounded childhood nor her husband, nor from the unmatched wounds they both carried from their past. Maybe they were searching for something elusive yet profound, a lost love, a home to settle their lost souls. Being older and wiser, Lamis understood her needs and what she had been searching for all these years. It was a soulmate, a love that would envelop her in its warm embrace and light the way to a brighter future, a guiding force to lead her home. Lamis clearly understood that the running child inside her hadn't yet found a home.

In her way of trying to find (her) peace, Lamis had to face society again, but this was not easy at all.

Generally, being a divorced woman in such a society is a shame for some and still is for others. She is considered easy prey. Lamis couldn't tell the closest people to her heart, not even her Aunty, since even she would not believe there to be any reason for the divorce unless she was physically abused, or else she'd be judged as the destroyer of the family. It wasn't easy to hide something like that from the only person who showed her love, yet she was sure that not doing so would break her heart. Her Auntie's death was the last thread that tied Lamis to her childhood memories; it was a tough loss indeed.

Her situation got worse when she tried to escape life itself. But God never let her down. He put a few beautiful souls in her path to bring her back strong and do something she wanted - her lovely sister and a spiritual mentor who just popped up. With their help, Lamis started focusing on what (really) mattered.

Passing through countless obstacles helped Lamis change her perception of life. Every morning, she thanked God that she and her loved ones were still in good health, both mentally and physically. She understands that life is short and never gets attached to anything tangible. She is not the only one in a country where hope is a rare commodity, dreams are imprisoned behind steel barriers, and aspirations are limited to basic survival instincts. In this environment, the only assurance one has is one's faith. Whenever Lamis felt down in the past, she returned to her memories of the colorful poppies she saw from the car window.

This time, she saw it from another perspective. She had to stay put. There was no escape this time since her mother's health had gotten worse, and it was her turn to stand beside her. Everything had changed, and her responsibilities were even greater than before.

Lamis now stands strong, no longer running or trying to escape. It is time to rise and fight, to take comfort in what was lost, and resolve insecurities. It is time to stand up and make peace with her surroundings. It's time to save her wounded spirit and, above all, create a home for her children by focusing on the window of opportunities and forget about the many closed doors.

Lamis believes that she is offering humanity two members whom she has to one day hand over to society, so no bullying or any physical or mental abuse, always maintaining communication, directing them when they feel lost, giving them the love they need, and appreciating all the blessings God gave.

The only escape she allows herself is to dig into stories to tell. Lamis finds significant characters to write about, remarkable people from history with whom she connects her wounds, dreams, desires, faith, and passion. She even shares some similarities, especially those on a quest for an extraordinary love story or a dream.

The runner wants to change something. She immerses herself in the stories of people's pain, drawn to the depths of their experiences, embracing their wounds, and uses it all to chart her (own) path in life, delving deep to uncover courage and resilience. One project that Lamis started working on, "Elissa, Queen of Tyre and Carthage," with her money, time, and effort, allowed her to participate in many events.

With the Beirut blast in Lebanon occurring, a revolution had already started. Due to an economic catastrophe and COVID-19, the project was devastated. With no money to continue and only waiting for solutions, this time, Lamis decides to benefit from this situation and continue her project by writing her novel and publishing it so as not to waste all the research and effort made after all those years.

She finally sees how a true queen can reign without running or escaping! Like Queen Elissa did. Lamis is trying to build her castle with its rooms, each one filled with its own beautiful story. For that, she is willing to welcome anything that helps her to feel safe and secure, embracing the 'stranger' she once was and giving the runner a path to walk that leads her to new open doors. By doing so, Lamis believes she can give hope to other 'stubborn,' 'strangers,' 'running girls' everywhere.

ABOUT THE AUTHOR

LAMIS CHKEIR

Lamis Chkeir is a mother of two kids, born and based in Beirut, Lebanon. She studied communication art at the American University of Science and Technology, where she earned her BA in audiovisual. Her passion for storytelling and visual arts propelled her to pursue further education at Saint Joseph University for her MA in cinematography, History, and International Relations. She has enhanced her global perspective and communication skills through participation in workshops, including those held by the Cannes Film Festival and Universal Pictures.

Lamis has worked in different international productions for years but found herself mainly working as a producer and writer. She started her career as an event organizer and presenter at a young age. After graduation, she established the communication field as a media representative, editor, documentary director, and other educational artistic works like symposiums and conferences.

As an executive producer, her last project was "BIGGER THAN US." A docu-film spanning eight countries and honored at the Cannes Film Festival Award and "Amour a 200 meter", a twenty-episode series filmed in RDC, for Canal+ TV.

As a writer, she published her novel "Elissa- Queen of Tyre and Carthage," a story that narrates the challenge of the courageous Elissa, known as Dido, a beloved Phoenician Queen who tirelessly fights for her people and establishes her new empire, Carthage. She was an example of intelligence, courage, and loyalty to humanity.

Lamis's work in the region creates an understanding and identification through the cultures that bring people closer together. She is writing her new novel to engage and inspire global audiences and executing a new documentary about the healers.

CHAPTER NINE

MY PUSH AND PRESS TO GREATNESS
BEVERLY LARUE (USA)

Going through any trauma can be devasting, so much so that it can leave a person in a state of feeling stuck, confused, confined, and all together, just not themselves anymore. These negative feelings can be challenging in every area of life long after the trauma is over. I understand this all too well due to my trauma from a brutal attack in 2012.

That trauma left me facing challenges that I faced continually. Nevertheless, my faith has given me an unmeasurable ability to rise above these challenges. Where the world might think that it's impossible to function at a high level of accomplishment after such a devasting attack on my life, my faith in God proved them wrong. Let me share a little bit of my story. I was brutally attacked and beaten with a hammer, and I was left for dead. My thumb was crushed, and my body had cuts and bruises on both knees. Not to mention, a close call from a boxcutter used to cut me from one ear to the other.

When I came home from the emergency room, this is something that I intensely remember. The attack was on a Monday. We had our Women Of Extreme Excellence (W.O.E.E.) ministry meeting in a few days. Even in my painful condition, I walked with a cane while still bruised and full of immense pain, with some of my body parts wrapped in bandages. I told myself I still must do what God called me to do. I must attend even if I don't stay at the book ministry.

As I walked in on my cane, I heard Pastor say, "I was coming because I knew Beverly was going to show up." That's a miracle. I knew what I was doing was for God, but I didn't realize the other people were watching my life this closely. I had to prove that my

GOD was still on the throne, taking care of me. And I was still about my Father's business despite my circumstances.

My first challenge was forgiveness. The Lord dealt with me about forgiveness, and I had to forgive my attacker. How can I so freely accept His forgiveness yet deny others to be forgiven?

One of the things He had me do was write a letter to my attacker telling him that I forgive him. Writing this letter was very difficult to understand, but I knew in my spirit that it would significantly impact my heart. After I wrote the letter and read it out loud, I felt the revelation of healing and wholeness in my heart.

It was as if the attack didn't happen! I knew it happened to my body, but the pain, sorrow, and heaviness of the remembrance were gone from my body. Our tissue and muscle remember the impact of trauma. But the remembrance was gone for me, or should I say lifted. Then God had me repeat this all day, every day. "No man has done me no wrong, and no man has done me no harm," I said this all day, every day for weeks and months. When I was sleeping, people would say, aren't you mad at him for doing this to you? In my heart, all I knew was that "No man had done me no wrong, and no man had done me any harm." Years later, it was revealed; I confessed that out loud and believed it in my heart. The root of bitterness could not take place and grow. Because if it did, it would have stopped what the Lord was doing in my life. The bitterness would not allow HIS love to flow and grow through me. This revelation helped me to heal in many areas of my life and relationships, even until today.

My next challenge was fear. After the attack, I was fearful of everything. I was afraid that I would be attacked again. I was terrified, scared, and uncertain about everything. What grounded me and assured me of my safety was my intimate relationship with GOD. He often reminded me that He would never leave or forsake me. The more I believed HIS WORD and trusted Him, the more I started going out of the house, from once every other week to two to three times a week alone. I spent hours reading the Bible and staying in HIS PRESENCE. I believed and trusted that the Lord would not let anything happen to me.

I read Psalms 91 all the time, and it reminded me that His angels are encamped around me to keep me from all harm. The more I read Psalms 91, the more my fear loosened its grip because of the power of GOD. The force of God's love pushed me to my greatness. That push allowed me to go above what I could imagine. I saw myself walking around and going in and out of places, ready to fulfill His purpose on earth.

The press and the pushing of this terrible situation was what God used to show me His greatness in me. We all have greatness in us. We must be ok with the awful, uncomfortable, painful situation only for a season. Then, I allowed the Lord to use my experience to show me the purpose for all that pain. It was not about me but about God's purpose for helping others reach their greatness through my experience. I realized that afterward, like giving birth, after the painful travail in childbirth, we forget the pain only to enjoy the new bundle of joy that arrived in our lives.

Being fragile and delicate was another one of my challenges. Just the sound of these words made me think of a weak person, but to me, after my trauma, these words I used to help myself, and others know how to handle me during my difficult times. The essence of my identity had shifted so much that I had to take it easy on myself. My whole thought process had to register new information about my emotional and mental capacity to handle daily tasks. Even the way I saw the world and how I responded to it.

By saying that, I felt fragile and delicate; I gave my voice authority and control over my state of being, not anyone else. Some days, I would look in the mirror and see the shell of the person that I was. I didn't even recognize myself, and it seemed like I had aged from my trauma. Through the weeks and months of therapy, I challenged myself, not against a date or psychological treatment, but against myself, against what I thought I could do. My God-given strength is what made the difference in my trauma. The Bible says in Joel 3:10, "When you are weak, say that you are strong." Yes, my body was hurt, cut, and bruised, but my inner being was just as strong, if not stronger. The Holy Spirit began telling me I was stronger than I thought. I started speaking the WORD of GOD over me every day. Some days, I had to wear headphones to stay in a good mental place.

I was determined to rise above this situation and knew this was not my end. My inner strength and determination gave me a powerful push and press to get in shape physically. I physically did exercises that I had never been able to do. My press for greatness was not only spiritual and mental, but now it was physical. I made a physical challenge that changed my physical appearance and my health. I started saying what God's word said about me. I confessed that I'm more than a conqueror (Rom. 8:37), and he causes me to triumph (2 Corin. 2:14). Speaking HIS WORD gave me the power to push past my physical limits to greatness. As you speak today, know that your words are your way out.

Your voice is your victory over your trauma; you can use it to clear your path to greatness. Each powerful word you speak about yourself becomes your reality as you believe it. You might not feel it, but you know you are destined for greatness. Your trauma can remind you about how strong you are. You were strong enough to go through the trauma and grow through it. Don't allow your trauma to stump your growth. An essential part of your growth is knowing that the trauma is what happened to your body. But it does not define who you are and who you will become. Know that you are free to be the new you that God created you to be. Use your voice to clear your steps on your Pathway To Trauma Recovery.

Not being able to trust was one of my major challenges from my trauma. I lost my ability to trust men and be alone with them. I felt threatened and unsafe in their presence. I did not know how to manage situations with men. My fear of being unsafe made me not trust them. Until the Lord told me not to let man pluck me out of his hands (John 10:8). This means no man can take me out of where He has me in Him. I am safe with the Lord and his angels. I believed that no man would hurt me, and God would set a safety standard for me (Isaiah 59:19). I began to believe every word the Lord said, and I stood on it. I could talk to male friends and, later on, build my strength by sitting alone with them.

Sometimes, I would wish that my earthly Father was here to protect me and help carry the burden of my trauma with me. He was so strong and always took care of me. The Lord gave me this analogy of feeling fatherless and how Jesus carried our burdens.

I am not comparing my earthly Father's life to my Heavenly Father. No one on this earth can compare to the true and living God. This is just how the Lord dealt with me.

My Heavenly Father wanted me to know that He understands to a degree about fatherlessness. Fix my gaze on HIM instead of man, my earthly Father. His Father turned away from Him on the cross not because of His sins but because of my sins. This is the scripture He gave me, Psalm 68:5, a father to the fatherless. This scripture lets me know that Jesus is with me in my situation. He is in His role as my Father and has not left me. And Isaiah 53:3, K.J.V. – He is despised and rejected of men; a man of sorrow, and acquainted with grief.

My Heavenly Father told me He was a human (man) with feelings. And that He understood my pain, sorrow, and grief. To be acquainted with something, you must know about it because you learned or experienced it. That scripture, right there, helped me so much. It made my healing more manageable and more bearable, knowing even though God, my Heavenly Father, sits on the throne. Jesus, His son, connects to my situation and circumstance, even if it was for a short time.

In my prayer time, Jesus gave me the example of Him through His death on the cross (for me). He shared this with me; He experienced Fatherlessness while on the cross for us. He is acquainted with a Father not being there in our darkest hour. The pain, disappointment, and sorrow and the tears that fell like blood. The heartache of loneliness and the anguish of a pain that breaks a daughter's heart when a Father is absent. A sudden absence leaves him asking, Father, why have you forsaken me? Even though it was only three days, it felt like an eternity. The thought of my Father turning from me hurt.

I went through this act of love for you, daughter so that you can have a relationship with my Father God. Going through the pit of hell and getting the keys to death was horrible. Not having my Father to protect me and guide me was forever etched in my mind and heart. Jesus understood the guidance needed in my life.

The abuse and torture at the hands of the very people my Father sent to protect me was unbelievable. The people that were supposed to accept me and love me. Instead, they wronged me. They seemed to want me around at times. Still, in their hearts, they had plans to abuse me and neglect me from receiving the proper care as a human being, from the beatings to spitting on me and the agonizing plucking of my beard, not to mention the beating of my flesh until my skin came off. Publicly naked and unashamed, the stares from people looking at me as if they wanted more pain infected on me. A pain they could never survive.

Not to mention the nails, oh, the nails. Remember that I was human, just as you are. Can you imagine how my flesh and bones felt with each bow of that hammer? It was as if my body was hollering through every one of my cells to stop. The agony, then another blow from the hammer. I felt all the pain, but at this point, my voice was faint, and the blood flooded my organs, which made speech difficult and breathing a struggle.

I was without strength from carrying that heavy wooden cross. The flogging left me lifeless at times, falling under the weight of a tree my Father created for His glory is now being used as a spectacle against His beloved son. He allowed birth into humanity, the same humanity I came to save to restore their relationship with my Father forever in eternity. While carrying that heavy cross, each step felt like my knees would burst and my ankles would break due to the severity of the beatings. Those who knew me looked at me as if they did not recognize me. My friends and followers looked at me with disbelief (in their hearts) that this whole ordeal was happening. My Mother's face was covered in pain, and her tears stained the road my blood was on.

The dear Mother, my Heavenly Father, gave me love and care, but He could not help me. The soldiers were so determined that I carried my (own) cross until they made someone standing in the crowd help me carry the cross. It seems as if He was watching in horror, demanding that he help me carry the cross. I'll never forget his face, looking at me eye to eye, wondering. Because I knew his thoughts, "Why, sis, did they beat Him so bad? He shared his strength with me. Every one of my steps was a little more bearable with his help. Being born into humanity with human feelings, I momentarily understood fatherlessness.

The feeling of disappointment, pain, shame, and hurt; most of all, I felt the void of my Father's presence (in my life). While my head hung, they pierced my side, thinking Father, please help me. I was given sour vinegar to the lips that blessed and healed them. The lips that told them that my Father loved them. Even the earth felt the dreadfulness of the act on my Father's son.

Now feeling fatherless, I looked up and with my breath said to my Father, forgive them, for they know not what they do. Then, those who hurt your son, forgive each person's hands that hurt me. Each person rallied to see me crucified. Because your love is in me, and your mercy and grace are for everyone. I asked my Father to forgive them for they know not what they do – Psalm 68:3 K.J.V.

Throughout all the challenges I have overcome, I would not have imagined all the greatness God placed in me. I look back over the years, starting with my 4DProductions as a playwright. From 2013 to 2024, I've written over thirty-five inspirational plays. And have performed more than 28 times on stage with some sold-out audiences. I have written my own songs, and I have my own soundtrack for my first performance in 2013. I was interviewed on Channel 7 News (Chicago) in 2019 for my stage play, "The New Me, I Didn't Want To Be," for Breast Cancer Month. Not including the many scripts still in plastic covers waiting for the appointed time.

I've been honored to perform for all ages and on many different topics in the South Suburban area of Illinois. I taught a six-week playwriting 101 course for children ages 9-17 at the Harvey Public Library. I've also presented a creative play for a six-week summer program for children ages 6-13. My cast has performed in schools, churches, senior living facilities, and local colleges.

I worked and performed with around sixty cast members over the past 12 years. I've been interviewed on the radio over a dozen times. Next, in 2021, I wrote my first book, "Divine Intimate Conversations," which is the journal of my conversations with the Lord. It's like a collection of love letters written from the heart of God. The words are like a melody from a song that only the reader and God know the words to. My intimate relationship with the Lord has changed my life so much that He wanted me to share it with the world. The next book was a collaboration with 13 women under the direction of Michael Bart Mathews, our manuscript development coach. All 13 women shared our healing journey from our earthly Father's (Good, bad, right, or wrong) involvement, or lack thereof, in our lives.

I was invited to tell my story inside the pages of this book with another group of thought leaders. This book allowed me to share how God walked me through my process of healing and wholeness. I know now that the Lord was opening and stretching the gifts He placed inside me before the creation. These are the things that were preordained before I was born. Today, I'm walking in my gifts, and they are manifesting in the natural. In 2023, although I am a playwright, the Lord shifted me into being an actress on stage. Sometimes, I would play small parts in my stage plays. But this time, He moved me into the place of being the main character. This was amazing, and I realized there is no limit to God's greatness in me.

It all started when one of my newest cast members kept telling me I was funny and we should do a skit together. At first, I thought to myself, not me. But everything fell into place once we came together and prayed for God's will. Sherita Jones made this comment that shaped my new character and gave life to my legacy through my last (Sir) name, "LaRue Street." Sherita said, Beverly, you've helped everyone else shine on stage. Now it's your time, it's all about you.

Full disclosure: Sherita did not exclude any cast members from participating. However, she understood I would not think of myself first because I always think about helping and serving other cast members to shine. Her warm, heartfelt statement allowed me to harness the power of my purpose by branching out and using more of my God-given talents. That's it, that's all.

Together, we created our very own comedy video. We were invited to perform at the Golden Dome in Chicago within one month of placing our video on Facebook. The audience loved us.

They laughed so hard and were amazed at how we presented Kawanza.

We were invited back to perform again at a later date. In March of 2024, I also had the opportunity to perform a skit entitled "The Grey Glory Social Club" for the Harvey, Illinois Park District for Seniors. After that performance, I was invited to perform at the Mayor's Office the following week and organize the real Grey Glory Social Club for Seniors. But no one wants to be grey! I'll change it to the "Glory Social Club.

Last but not least, my latest Black History play, "Black History is Everywhere, Everyday All The Time," was a sold-out performance. In that play, I was the main character. The cast was amazing, and that's when I realized I enjoyed being on stage more. There is a scripture near and dear to my heart, and I stand by it today – "Greater is He that is within me than he that is in the world – 1 John 4:4 KJV. I used to be scared to say that I'm great. I didn't want to seem arrogant. Until one day, the Lord gave me the revelation of using this word correctly.

He said you are great because greater life is inside of you. I thought, "Greater is He that is within me than he that is in the world – 1 John 4:4 KJV. Then, I began to walk into my greatness after each push and press of God. Today, right now, you have greatness in you. You've already been pushed and pressed because you are here reading this book. I pray that your thoughts about your challenges change into a positive push and press into your greatness.

May my words echo in your heart, then reach into the depths of your soul to manifest your greatness. A greatness that your trauma can not cut off, destroy, or delay. Your trauma was just the path God used for your greatness. Now is the time to share it with the world and empower others to continue to push and press into their greatness. Our challenges have brought about a change that will change the world, one person at a time, on the Pathway To Trauma Recovery.

It's your time! I'm here for you, and you are not alone. There is no need to suffer in silence. Help is available for you, just like it is available for me. It's time to get serious and start on your journey of finding your moment of clarity and discover your power within.

Beverly LaRue

ABOUT THE AUTHOR

BEVERLY LARUE

Beverly LaRue, founder of Women of Extreme Excellence Ministries since 2007. Named by God, He said, "These women have been through the extreme in life, and they will be excellent unto me." In 2011, W.O.E.E. shifted to develop a book ministry that the Lord orchestrated.

She taught and spoke during the monthly meetings. Beverly LaRue joined her spiritual foundation at Abounding Life Church of God in Christ, where she was on the hospitality committee and helped with children's programs.

In 2012, the Lord gifted Beverly to dictate as He spoke. He called her a "Divine Dictator". Her first gospel stage play, "Secret Love" (John 15:13), debuted November 2, 2013, with a sold-out audience at Prairie State College, Chicago Heights, Illinois. Beverly has her first soundtrack for Secret Love to accompany the play.

Mystery Kingdom (Hebrews 11:6) was her second gospel stage play, which debuted May 30, 2015, at the S.P.A.A. Theater, Park Forest, Illinois. She is working on her book with a workbook for teaching kingdom relationships. This play included her first self-written song, "Love Drew Us to Seek the Master, " and her first personal soundtrack recording.

The Lord has used her life as an example of His Love and Grace. Since then, Beverly has worked with two other playwrights and performed her first thirty-minute play, "See Me Through My Daddy's Eyes," February 5-6, 2016, at Prairie State College. For

His glory, the Lord put her in a place that pressed her towards purpose.

In May 2016, Beverly performed a dramatization, "Calling For The Cunning Women," at the Corner Stone House of God Church in Harvey, Illinois, for their Women's Day Celebration. On May 7, 2016, she performed a play, "Kingdom Women Are Created."

Beverly performed a solo skit, "Through Love and Grace," Based on the scripture, Psalms 51:10, at a Mother's Day Tea given at Our Treasures Consignment Shop, Hazel Crest, Illinois. In 2016, the play "Love Gathering" was birthed, and she performed. "With love and kindness have I drawn thee" was the theme.

The Lord is healing His people's hearts back to Him. Beverly hosted a Father's Day Event on June 19, 2016, at Orland Park Civic Center, where her cast performed two stage plays that night. The first play was "Jr. Defense," and the second was "The Father's Impact". The audience was surprised to have dinner and two complete plays filled with messages to the fathers reinforcing their value to their family, church, and community.

On October 22, 2016, the cast performed "Connections," which stands for Connecting Others Needs & Navigating Empowering Connections through Individuals & Organized Network Systems. In 2017, Beverly had the honor of teaching a playwriting class to children ages 9-15 for four weeks at the Harvey Public Library. The climax was the children performing their (own) written stage play "Book World" with a red carpet photo shoot and certificates of completion.

Her next adventure was providing a "Creative Play" for the "Carriage House" summer program for six weeks. She taught children ages 6-10 how to have fun acting by incorporating role-playing into their daily activities. Their class concluded with a final "Carriage House Superhero's" performance.

In 2017, Beverly became a member of S.P.A.A. and STAT. In 2018, her presentation, "Use Your Pencil To Meet People With

Passion," Master playwriting class at S.P.A.A. In 2019, she wrote a play, "The New Me, I Didn't Want To Be," for Breast Cancer Month. That performance provided her with an interview on Channel 7.

In 2021, she wrote her first book "Divine Intimate Conversations." This book was her journal that she wrote in the presence of the Lord, as He would speak to her. Those conversations were intimate and private, yet loving for all the world to hear of HIS indescribable love. She co-authored the #1 New Release and #2 Bestseller Daddy Daughter Dynamics under the coaching of Michael Bart Mathews.

Her humor lit up the stage when she played in the skitcom, "LaRue Street," created in 2023. "LaRue Street" performed at the Golden Dome in Chicago less than two months after the first performance. In 2024, Beverly was pushed to her greatness by performing solo comedy skits for seniors in the community at Harvey's mayor's office.

Beverly LaRue
Email: blarue.2024 @gmail.com
Direct number: 1-708-530-1437

CHAPTER TEN
'BEAUTY FOR ASHES'
DELPHINE LYN HARRIS

Isaiah 61:3a

"To appoint unto them that mourn in Zion, to give unto them

BEAUTY for ASHES."

Birth to 20 yrs.

'Ashes'

Let me begin by saying our family lived in a house with an additional apartment in the back where my mother and father allowed family members who had nowhere to live. My family attended Faith Temple Church of God in Christ. Both parents were active members and professed Jesus as Lord in their lives. My father was a boxer, and my mother a nurse, but Lonnie Lee would every day find a reason to be abusive to my mother and us children. I think it was because he was an only child without a father to call dad. In comparison, my mother was raised with a mother and father. I think he was angry at his mother but took it out on my mother.

My mother, Mae A. Harris, and my father, Lonnie L. Harris, had five children, including twin girls (Celestine and Delphine). After she gave birth to twins (me and my sister), she admitted to her husband, Lonnie Lee, that Delphine may be Benny's child. My oldest sister moved out of the house at age 16, marrying an older man. After graduation, my oldest brother enrolled in the Air Force, leaving George and the twins at home. As you know, sometimes you are in some situations driven into another man's arms for compassion, comfort, and love, but went back to her husband, and they became sexually involved immediately...I know it may seem impossible, but I was the child of another man (Mr. Benny Harris), while my twin sister was biologically the child of (Mr. Lonnie L. Harris).

Studies show that, in rare cases, fraternal twins can be born from two different fathers in a phenomenon called heteropaternal superfecundation. Although uncommon, rare cases have been documented where a woman is pregnant by two different men at the same time. To figure out if this is the case, a DNA paternity test can be done after the birth of the twins. At the same time, the woman is pregnant to determine if the twins have different fathers – as stated and medically reviewed by Layan Airhmani, M.D., ob-gyn, MFM. (Written by Irina Gonzalez, July 28, 2021).

How heteropaternal superfecundation occurs:

It occurs when a second egg is released during the same menstrual cycle. That egg needs to be fertilized by the sperm of a different man during sex that takes place in a short period from the time that the first egg was fertilized, 12-24 hours (timeline can be extended) from the release of an egg.

Paternity testing after twins are born: One way to determine if twins have different fathers is with a paternity test after the twins are born.

After 73 years of wondering if I had the same mother and father (my mother told me that my twin sister and I had different fathers), I felt emptiness during my childhood, adolescence, and adult years. Here, I suggest if you are a twin and you have second thoughts about parental identity, I highly recommend you submit a DNA test while your parents and twin are alive. Both of my parents were deceased during my DNA testing. The many questions I want to ask my parents, except for the DNA test results, will never be answered. Yes, the test is the next best thing. However, I'm 73 (at the time of this publication), with many unanswered thoughts, questions, and emotional feelings that will linger until I leave this earth.

The DDC-DNA Diagnostics Center did my DNA testing/reporting to determine the siblingship of my twin sister and me. Based on testing results obtained from analyses of the DNA listed, the probability of full siblingship is 99.6%. The likelihood that they share the same biological father is 332 to 1. After reading the test results, I felt free because I already knew my sister was my twin, and after 73 years, I finally knew I was Lonnie Lee, my father's daughter.

As stated earlier, my parents were active in the Church. I remember my mother saying while she was pregnant with my sister and me (twins), she received the gift of the Holy Ghost (a Spiritual Gift from God - Acts 2:4, "And they were all filled with the Holy Ghost/Spirit, and began to speak with other tongues, as the Spirit gave them utterance). We have been anointed all our lives, discerning the Spirit in people, places, and things. The devil has tried his best to kill both of us.

Celestine suffered from Anemia (a condition in which the blood doesn't have enough healthy red blood cells), and my sister was given a blood transfusion every day to stay alive. I suffered from Asthma (a long-term inflammatory disease of the airways of the lungs). It was so bad that I had to sleep in a tent because of my wheezing twenty-four hours daily, keeping everyone up all day and night. I also had Eczema (a skin condition that causes the skin to become red, itchy, and inflamed). It is a disease having scales so bad that there were dark sores all over my body from scratching day and night because of the itching.

One night, God healed me at age eight while visiting my grandmother (Mariah Fitzpatrick) in Hardaway, Alabama. Grandmothers had those old remedies. She told me to urinate in this cup and drink it. At first, I fought to drink it, but my grandmother made me, and I did. Immediately, the *wheezing* stopped, and the *itching* stopped. HALLELUJAH!

When we were younger, as time passed, I remember our family owning a restaurant named Harris Duckin on Hasting St. and 12th in Detroit, Michigan. I also remember the Chrysler Corporation came into our black neighborhoods, offering money to buy out black business owners and wanted them to work for them. Most black business owners took Chrysler up on their offer. My father took the offer and began working for Chrysler in Detroit, Michigan. As time passed, my father was transferred to Akron, Ohio, and (our) family moved with him. Mom stayed in Detroit and continued working at Harper Hospital. She didn't want to quit her job if things in Akron didn't work out. **Mom was a Wise Woman.**

Continuing with my story, I was the second twin who was not favored or liked because of my color. Since I wasn't the child of Lonnie Lee…my life was and was not a Cinderella story. I was told to go to bed after school. I only ate leftover food if there was anything left after each meal. I never received lunch money, so I was always hungry and looking for food. Despite my inhumane treatment, I was a <u>straight-A student</u> throughout Elementary and Junior High School. I remember being in the 5th grade at Jennings High School while living with Lonnie Lee in Akron, Ohio. We weren't allowed to participate in field trips or school-sponsored special events. We had to be placed in another class while our 5th grade enjoyed outside events and trips. I was placed in this 6th-grade class, and a complex math problem was put on the board. Within minutes, I figured out the problem, which allowed me to be promoted to the 6th grade. I received no congratulations, praise, love, affection, or encouragement from my parents for my accomplishment. I was assertive, and my twin sister Celestine was passive. I always felt rejected by both parents.

We traveled between Detroit, Michigan, and Akron, Ohio, on weekends because my mother had to work late and could not care for us. As time passed, my dad wanted us to return to Detroit and live with my mother. After school was out in the summer of 1964, we moved back to Detroit to live with our mother.

We didn't graduate from the Akron educational system because we transferred back to school in Detroit. We began classes at Webber Junior High. After graduating, I attended Northwestern in the 10th grade. I moved with my oldest sister. It was good for a while, but my sister couldn't afford to care for me. I had to move back in with my mother and continue attending Northeastern High. When you haven't been loved by your father or the man who cared for you, it's hard not to fall for any young man interested in you.

In my senior year in high school, I met Woodrow J. Randle at a party. He was twenty-eight, and I was seventeen years old. I wasn't supposed to be at that party! I climbed out the bedroom window, went to my friend's party, and had a great time. Woodrow was there for me throughout my senior year without pressuring me to have sex. In my mind, this was the first man who (really) cared for me. I graduated from high school with honors. At age eighteen, my sister received a car, and I received nothing from either parent. It did not matter because I was IN LOVE with Woodrow. Young love is compelling! I'm sure, my dear readers, you remember!

I was thinking because Woodrow never pressured me for sex and was always good to me, I thought, why not? He took me to a hotel, and we had sex one time. One time is all it took to get pregnant. When I told Woodrow of my pregnancy, he was happy. He promised me marriage, a house, and to be my husband. During my pregnancy, everything was great between us. We picked out wedding rings, set a date to get married, and looked at what would be our newlywed home. I was on cloud nine, and I was feeling fine.

As time passed, I met Woodrow at his brother's house, where I thought he lived. One day, I was able to get his wallet, and I saw the address of where he lived. The license address differed from the address where we kept meeting. I became curious to know if I was lied to. I went to the address and saw Woodrow walking out of his house with a little boy sitting around his neck, getting into a car while another woman was coming out. This shocked and devastated me. Again, I was disappointed by another man who lied and used me.

I wanted to kill myself, and I wanted to drive off the bridge of Belle Island in Detroit.

I PRAYED FIRST… a still, small voice said no…instead, I went home and cried all night. I was so hurt and ashamed I didn't want to tell my mother. Around midnight, because I was so upset, my water broke, and I began having labor pains. I called out to my mother in the room next to mine. She asked me for Woodrow's address and phone number. I gave her the address but didn't have the phone number. It was raining hard when we arrived at Lincoln Park Hospital. While the nurses prepared me in the labor room…, my mother and sister went to Woodrow's address and announced

I was having his baby. Within a few hours, I gave birth to my daughter, Felicia Lyn, was born.

Woodrow never came to see me in the hospital. When my Mother looked for Woodrow the next day to ask if he was coming to see me, to her surprise, everything was gone, and his house was empty. For the next eighteen years, I raised Felicia Lyn without help or knowing where her father, Woodrow, lived. To my surprise, after eighteen years of not hearing or knowing where Woodrow had gone, he called to see how I was doing. I said, "You got the nerve" to contact me after abandoning me and your daughter eighteen years ago. I felt so enraged, and I hung up the phone. He contacted his daughter, Felicia Lyn, to build a relationship.

Eighteen years ago, after giving birth, my daughter, my twin sister Celestine, and I moved to the Projects off John C. Lodge and Forrest St., in a two-bed apartment. Beginning living life as we thought we could. Two other young women moved in to help with rent and bills. I remember one of the other young women and I met a band member who saw us dancing. Ask us if we want to travel as part of their show. We said yes, and I asked Celestine if she would care for Felicia while I pursued this adventure. We traveled and danced exotic for about a year. Trouble occurred with the band from selling drugs. We left and were homebound. It was an adventure to travel from City to City, State to State, and be able to dance, dance, dance!

20 years to 40 years

The next phase of my life was more traumatic. As I share this part of my story, I reflect on how trusting I was and how easily that trust shattered how I felt. Here we go. I met another guy named Rose. He said all the right things that a woman wanted to hear. So, I felt comfortable enough to go out with Rose, especially after experiencing the lies, cheating, and fatherless absenteeism that Woodrow put me through with the birth of my lovely daughter. I needed a real man to step up and be a man. So, Rose took me on a date, and he raped me. I could not stop him because he overpowered me. I did not believe what was happening to me. I began to cry tears of disbelief, sadness, and pain.

I never saw Rose again after he raped me, but the memory of his horrific actions lingered in my mind. I developed deep trust issues with men. About a month after I was raped, I became pregnant for the second time. After finding out the news, I wanted to get an abortion. I decided to tell my mother that I was going to get an abortion. I went to New York to have the abortion, but unbeknownst to me, I was too far along with my pregnancy. The doctor said, Delphine, you must remain in the hospital for three days. My mother's prayers were answered! We were Christians, and she didn't want me to abort the baby because she did not believe in abortions. After nine months, I gave birth to my second daughter, Titania Mae. I'm 22 years old and have two children. Raising two children as a single parent, with neither father being around for help, was a very challenging experience. By the Grace of God, I managed. I had no choice but to realize my position in life and do whatever it took (legally and morally) to raise my babies.

Time passed, and my children were getting older. I had the opportunity to audition for the position on the NBA's Detroit Pistons Cheerleading squad at age 27. I auditioned and became one of the Detroit Pistons' cheerleaders in 1979. Being accepted as an NBA Detroit Pistons Professional Cheerleader was an exciting time for me to be a part of something good. This phrase in my life was fulfilling a childhood dream. My father, Benny, came with Mom to one of the games to see me perform. I was excited that my father came. However, we never had a father-daughter relationship. My father died soon afterward. During the 1979 season, when I was cheerleading, some of the Detroit Pistons' players were Bob Lanier, John Long, Terry Tyler, Kevin Porter, and M.L. Carr, among other outstanding team members.

The following year, 1980, I met another man, William J. Williams. Now mind you, my devasting rape experience with Rose was still on my mind. However, I knew I could not isolate myself for the rest of my life. I worked at a law firm as the receptionist at Dyer, Meek, Rugesagger, and Bullard in Detroit. William opened the door and said, 'I'm gonna marry you one day.' He sent me flowers and a message for the girls and me; lunch was on him. Again, a man showing interest in me was what I needed in my life. William eventually became my husband, which made me happy because I could trust men (again). William turned out to be a gangster and a loan shark. Being a sheltered church girl, this lifestyle was exciting but dangerous.

The first two years of being married to William were good. But after two years in this marriage, I had to work and give my husband, Willian, my paycheck. He spent the money I made and gave me what he thought I needed to keep my hair and appearance up to suit him. I was so miserable, and I felt like a failure once again. I returned to God, asking him to forgive me and get me out of this marriage. My husband had other women along with me at home. The things I saw him do to others were devastating. I wondered how I got into a relationship and then a marriage with an evil man like William.

As time went on, I decided to leave William. I left, and I hid out at my mom's. I was scared for my life because I witnessed the mental, physical, and emotional abuse he inflicted on others. William knew where to find me. He came to my mom's house and kicked the front door down. My husband ran upstairs, put me over his shoulder, and took (kidnapped) me back to Gallagher St., where we were living before I ran away. He gave my mother money to have the door fixed. William took me to the basement and shouted, "You belong here with me. If you try and leave again, I will cut you up and put you in this freezer."

I prayed. I put holy oil on William's pillar, shoes, and clothes all over the house, cabinets, and furniture. I kept praying, LORD, I need you to get me out of here. One night, after my husband stayed out drinking and partying, he came home and told me to get my daughters and get out. I couldn't leave fast enough. It was a prayer answered. We soon divorced, and I was free. THANK YOU, JESUS! My trust in men was at an all-time low. However, my Faith, Hope, Love, and Trust in God were at an all-time high.

As time passed, I was now thirty-three. I should be somewhat wiser as time moves on, right? He had the same name as my last husband, so I will call him Red so as not to confuse you. Well, let's continue the story, my dear readers. I met another man, William (Red) Manson, a carpenter and a Church going guy. I met

Red at my Church, and he was very attentive to me. He cooked, cleaned, and was good for me. I met Red's sister, who had a house for sale on Whitcomb in Detroit. He bought it before we married and told me this is a present/gift from me to you. We soon married because, in my mind, this was the perfect marriage from God. Again, after two years of marriage with Red, the bathroom door was closed one night. We didn't close the doors, so I opened the door, and surprise, surprise! Red had an illness that he didn't tell me about, which made me furious. When we talked about this illness, he would get mad at me because I didn't want to have anything else to do with him. Again, my trust was broken, and we were divorced.

40 years to 60 years

Okay, here's where my wrong choice of men continued. I met another guy named Isaiah Wimbley when I was forty-five when I worked for a businessman. Isaiah needed to discuss a business transaction with the owner. He smiled and asked for my phone number. Isaiah was younger than me; however, we clicked regardless of age. He showed me another side of life, and shortly afterward, we married. I felt that this marriage was the one that will work. Long story short, my third husband was very possessive and controlling. He was so possessive and controlling that he monitored everything I did. When I went to work, Isaiah would call me all day long to check on what I was doing. My husband's actions made me feel wanted and cared for, okay. At least that's what I thought. In my third marriage, I regretted my husband because he was Dr. Jekyll at Church but Mr. Hyde at home. At Church, everyone considered him the perfect spouse. But at home, he treated me like a child. I had to do as he said and nothing else. I did not want to live with this man for the rest of my life. After two years of marriage, we divorced because I was not going to accept another man who did not know how to treat a woman.

I've been married three times at this stage in my life. After all these years, to my surprise, I met and reconnected with my childhood sweetheart at the Fox Theater in Detroit. I knew Frank from attending the Lighthouse Tabernacle Church, where everybody is welcome. Frank R. Patrick was now a successful businessman, owning several eighteen-wheeler trucks. I loved Frank from age twelve. Tell me this wasn't God finally giving me the right mate. We rekindled our love, attended Church, and sat on the front row as members for about two years. We were the best-dressed couple wherever we went, and we also loved to dance. When we graced the dance floor, all eyes were on us. We were like the black Ginger Rogers and Fred Astaire. There was nothing too complex or challenging we didn't overcome. Our children would come to our home at Easter, Christmas, Thanksgiving, Memorial Day, and July 4, and we would always have a good time. This was what I always wanted in a marriage. And yes, to my surprise, he began to go out without me after a while. He kept telling me that he wanted some time alone.

This man worked driving from state to state, came home, got in bed and slept till midnight, got up, took a shower, and left me. Our travels were to his parents' home in the two years we were married. He never took me out of town to see the sites when he was not working. We saw sites only when he had a trip in his truck. I tell you, my life has been nothing but HELL in these four marriages.

First, it was Woodrow, the fatherless father of my first daughter. Second, it was Rose, the man who raped me and the fatherless father to my second daughter. Third, it was William, my first husband, the loan shark and gangster, who threatened to cut me up and put my body parts in an ice box. Red and my second husband kept secrets from me. I have always kept my faith, hope, and love for God—My third husband, Isaiah Wimbley, was possessive and a controller, and Frank R. Patrick, my fourth husband, was the user. After all my past experiences:

"I'M STILL ON TOP," LADIES, IT PAYS TO WAIT AND LET GOD CONFIRM WHO IT IS HE HAS FOR YOU

60 years to Present Day

Before my mother, Mae Arthur Harris-Moore, passed at 81 in 2004, she married again for about two years to Mr. Moore, who was abusive also. My twin sister and I followed our mother's patterns. She asked the other twin to (come) get her. My sister was the caregiver for my mom for about ten years. Our mother died from Alzheimer's disease, but when we viewed her body, she looked like an angel lying in the casket. There was calm PEACE on her face that let me know she was at REST IN HEAVEN.

Before Lonnie Lee's death at 94, our recovery would come to pass. My brother, Michael, and I would visit him three times a year. I needed to see him because of the Love of God in my heart. After a while, Lonnie Lee became ill because he did not take proper care of himself. While at the gas station pumping gas, Lonnie Lee blacked out. He was rushed to the hospital. The hospital called me because he had kept my business card in his wallet. The doctor asked me to talk to him. Lonnie Lee's first words were, "come get me." Without hesitation, I called my brother to meet me and asked my daughter to come with me to catch the bus.

We arrived in Montgomery, Alabama, where Lonnie Lee lived. We packed everything in his Cadillac and were homebound to Detroit, where he stayed with me for seven months. We talked about everything that had made me angry. We went to Church, went shopping, and renewed our relationship. While Lonnie Lee was staying with me, he came across the scripture, Matthew 20:16, *"So the last be first, and the first last; for many be called, but few chosen."* Lonnie Lee asked me to have an attorney come to the house and make out a will, leaving me money and his car. He went to stay with my twin sister. After two months, Lonnie Lee had a double stroke, remained in the hospital for five months, and died. When we viewed his body in the casket, he looked like he did as a boxer. There was a calm peace on his face that let me know he was at REST IN HEAVEN.

<u>*'Beauty'*</u>

Isaiah 61:3a says, "To appoint unto them that mourn in Zion, to give unto them BEAUTY for ASHES."

Queen aka Delphine

As I complete this final chapter for this collaboration project, I am single at 73 years young and HAPPY! Let me make this (<u>perfectly</u>) clear: "This is not the final chapter in my life; I'm just getting started."

I'm in my **Seventies…** by the GRACE OF GOD.

I have listed a few accolades that make me smile EVERY DAY.

Matthews 6:4: "That thine alms may be in secret: and thy Father which seeth in secret himself shall reward thee openly."

In 2021, when I turned seventy, True Johnson of Detroit told me, "God wants me to give you a TEA," calling it 'The Queen's Tea. 'I'm called 'Queen by GOD.' Let me share my testimony. Over 20 years ago, in a Prayer meeting with a Team of Women called 'The Prayer Posse,' which I was a part of…. the Holy Ghost called me out and changed my name to Queen. In 2007, at a Prophetic Conference, the meeting host called and reminded me who the Lord had called me. HALLELUJAH !!!

It pays to **OBEY GOD…..** at this Tea (over 150 individuals witness a monetary gift presented by Pastor Art Cartwright of Global–Empowerment Ministries in Detroit. This ministry has helped empower black business owners to get their products on the shelves of stores, outlets, and shopping malls. As of January 2024, over 400 black-owned businesses from this ministry are thriving and providing. TO GOD BE THE GLORY…Thank You, and PRAISE THE LORD.

In 2022 and 2023, during my birthday celebration blessings in Detroit and Walled Lake, Michigan. Pastor Bishop Hugh D. Smith referred to me as "She sets the <u>STANDARD</u>." The daughter of Pastor (Bethany) blessed me with a pair of <u>RED BOTTOM</u> shoes. My granddaughter (Mariah) blessed me with a trip <u>PAID IN FULL</u> to Miami, Florida. My spiritual daughter (Octavia) blessed me with a <u>CRYSTAL</u> necklace. My friend's mother (Christine) blessed me with <u>TWENTY PAIR OF SHOES</u>. I was featured as a cousin in the movie – The Fakers.

Now, this is where it gets better. I received a text message from the Kia car dealership on Wednesday, June 21, 2023. That Friday, I drove out of the dealership with a <u>BRAND NEW 2023 KIA FORTE.</u> OMG!

My Christian sister (Dr. Liz) selected me as part of her <u>BOARD OF DIRECTORS</u> for her Soothing Salve all-natural herbs product business. Her salves relieve sore muscles and stiffness, reduce pain, and fight inflammation for better performance. And to put the icing on the cake, Dr. Liz, creator of Soothing Salve, and Coach Michael Bart Mathews, creator of We Create Books, invited me to become a published author in this extraordinary literary book project with a group of phenomenal writers from several countries. Because of this opportunity, I can tell my story and get my chapter out of my head so it can be published and read. Now **It's Smoothie Time** because while you are **Finding Your Moment of Clarity: Discovering Your Power Within,** inside the pages of this book, our mission is to empower you to **Harness The Power of Purpose** and become the BEST YOU.

I want to SHOUT OUT and encourage you to reread our stories, stand on our shoulders, and PURSUE YOUR GOALS AND DREAMS! If we, the coauthors in this book, can do it, so can you. You are not alone.

Delphine Lyn Harris

ABOUT THE AUTHOR

DELPHINE LYN HARRIS

Delphine Lyn Harris is a Prayer Warrior, Minister, Liturgical Worship (praise dancer), Mother of two daughters, Grandmother of eight, Great-grandmother of six and a twin. She has been an entrepreneur her entire life. Delphine is a third-generation business owner and loves it.

She began as an independent consultant for Swarovski Touchstone Crystal. Delphine is currently an investor partner, a board member of Soothing Salve, and an image consultant for women. She's in the process of opening an Adult Daycare Center for adults with disabilities. Her center will have an on-site ice cream parlor where residents can enjoy a delicious treat while enjoying the day's activities.

Delphine was educated at Northeastern High School and Detroit, Michigan Business Institute before striking out on her own. She has been a stenographer, computer programmer for a regional office manager, statistical office manager, food/recovery coordinator, municipal property tax processor, and counter clerk in Southfield, Michigan. She is a dynamo outside of work. Delphine led a monthly one-hour Prayer group in Southfield, Michigan, for fifteen years to the present day. She has performed the liturgical dance for over twenty years in Detroit to the present day. She's a volunteer usher at the Fox Theater in Detroit for nine years and an Usher for the Detroit Grand Prix for seven years to the present day.

Delphine was nominated and Awarded on Saturday, October 2023, by Hannah Center in Detroit for those over Seventy who are committed to a cause. Also, at 28, in 1997, over 5,000 participants auditioned to become an NBA Detroit Pistons Cheerleader. Delphine and young women aged eighteen to twenty-one were selected as one of the finalists. She was elated to be the oldest but placed as one of the 24 members chosen for the squad HOORAY. In June of 2023, viewed in a Commercial at Embassy Covenant International Church, Senior Pastor Bishop Hugh D. Smith, for the Human Dignity Awards service of men and women who worked tirelessly, often away from the limelight, driven by pure commitment to a cause they believe in.

As a member of Embassy Covenant Church International, in June 2014, Bishop Hugh D. Smith spoke into her life…God has given you Beauty for Ashes." The Lord has guided Delphine to become a contributing Author by submitting her content for our "Path To Tramua Recovery" book project.

Delphine Is Available for engagements:

1 (313) 204-1607 or 1 (313) 712-1301
Email: idelphinep@gmail.com
rainbowadultdaycareharris@gmail.com
Facebook:
https://www.facebook.com/profile.php?id=61558763451414
Website:
https://idelphinep.wixsite.com/imdoingmenow-1
Instagram:
https://www.instagram.com/iamdoingmenow

CHAPTER ELEVEN
FROM A CATERPILLAR
TIMMY YOUNG (USA)

<u>MY ROOTS</u>

The 'pecking order' of a family is sometimes a mystery, but I have always understood my role as the fifth child and third son of six children growing up in a small town in Oklahoma. Of course, many will say that Shawnee isn't a small town for Oklahoma, but that's when you know you're talking to an actual Oklahoman. Shawnee is a town of less than 35,000 people located around thirty-five miles east of Oklahoma City, with nine elementary schools, one junior high, and one high school when I was growing up. Our community always had the 'big fish in a small pond' mentality.

<u>THE FAMILY FOUNDATION</u>

I was born to Carl and Betty Young one month after the Civil Rights Bill of 1964 was signed into law by President Lyndon B. Johnson. Next to my relationship with the Almighty God, my family is the most important thing in my life, and I feel the most satisfied in their presence. I make excuses to be with them by hosting events and attending as many family gatherings as possible. Being there is important, but it's also what I take away from each conversation that is so satisfying as I learn from others.

As the fifth child in my family, I have a pretty cool observation point to see how things are done in a family with plenty of help from those who walked before me, leading the way to how our parents wanted to groom us. We shared lots of love, the kind of love that wasn't spoken directly, but you knew it was there and not going anywhere. That is part of what helped develop me into who I am today: a man after God's heart, a believer, and a Renaissance man.

My parents were high school sweethearts who began their family as teenagers. Their focus was always on God and their children.

They ensured we were clean, dressed nicely, and had food in our stomachs. We were taught from the King James version of the Bible. To this day, I greet my mother on the phone with, "How Art Thou?"

In 1974, my mother became the first Black female pastor in Pottawatomie County, Oklahoma, against the acceptance of other religious leaders who all assumed she was serving the devil because "women weren't supposed to lead church!" Well, she didn't just lead a church. She led many people into a relationship with our Heavenly Father. After 40+ years, she never understood why it mattered whether it was a male or a female tongue delivering the message of Hope. She gave Hope to many people, and I'm one of them, to walk by faith, and we are better today because of her leadership.

Daddy was a "do it all" person who never met a stranger or a hammer that he didn't like. He was a great athlete at segregated Dunbar High School. My Dad played football and basketball and was selected as an All-State student-athlete in both sports. He also performed well in the carpentry class and (over the years) continued to help community members who needed repairs or additions to their houses until his health slowly deteriorated. Fortunately, that couldn't keep the ever-present smile off his face. He once said he had a punt return touchdown called back while playing football because he roughed the punter. He was extremely fast; however, this story never passed the 'sniff test' although many of his stories were later validated by family and friends who witnessed his skills.

I am incredibly thankful for the many lessons I learned from my older siblings. They taught me about the standards in our family, and they demonstrated by example the correct way of doing each detail of each chore. We didn't have male or female chores since we all had two legs and hands appropriately placed on our bodies. The girls took out the trash, and the boys washed dishes.

Most importantly, I learned what NOT to do by watching what the older ones did or didn't do correctly the first time. I learned to cry (quickly) when being disciplined. I learned not to use Daddy's tools without asking for permission and never pick up my little brother by the neck. Like in many communities across the country, we all inherently learned to go into the house when the streetlights came on, or a parent would soon be at the door as a reminder.

Back then, we had fruit trees in our yard: plum, pear, peach, apple, and a blackberry bush. We also had a garden, so I don't remember being hungry as a child. Mason Jars were part of our lives; we were like ants; we stored up for the next season. Dinner at the table was our gathering time to come together (not only for food) and connect as a family in meaningful conversations.

I didn't speak much because the youngest had the least amount of information, so it was an educational time for me. I vaguely remember the seating arrangement. I always seemed to be in the middle between Mama and Terry. Daddy was always at the head of the table and said the blessing over the food. Gwen and Carla were on the opposite side while Rickey occupied the end of the table. Side note: how do we get a head and an end of a table? Meals were always hot unless we had ball practice and got home after dinner was served.

My family is loving, and we are all peacekeepers and peacemakers. We embrace one another and those who enter our presence with love, joy, peace, and a big smile to make you feel welcome. We are so much better as a family because of this attitude of loving one another, accepting those who are different, and not holding on to the past. 'Blessed are the peacemakers, for they shall be called the children of God.' Matt 5:9.

I am a child of the Living God with one big desire: for all my friends to meet all my friends. I believe we (who are) peacekeepers will come together to create a network of peacekeepers—a community filled with people who want to be friendly, trusted, and trustworthy. Knowing my identity is key to keeping the momentum going as I serve others. Treating others the way I want to be treated is not always easy, but I'm not doing it for humans. My goal is to do the will of my Heavenly Father. It's not just a slogan but a destination for me: be the change I want to see in this world.

<u>**MY EDUCATIONAL JOURNEY**</u>

I attended kindergarten at Dunbar Elementary School before finishing my early years at Washington Elementary School, then on to Shawnee Jr. High and Shawnee High School. I graduated as Senior Class President and as an All-State football player. I continued my education at Oklahoma State University on a football scholarship, coached by Jimmy Johnson and his infamous staff, before transferring to East Central University in Ada, Oklahoma. There, I majored in Criminal Justice with a minor in Military Science and was an Alpha Phi Alpha Fraternity, Inc member.

It was common for me to be around large groups of people in football, the military, the fraternity, and as a student-athlete on campus. There was always someone to hang out with and share life experiences. I later returned to ECU to complete my Master's in education administration, and I've been an educator since 1995. I've served thousands of students and countless nationalities from all over the world.

I tease that I learned how to be a sneaky criminal at East Central University. I use the term "sneaky criminal" in the context of the following section. I was far from being a criminal element that anyone had to fear during my college days.

<u>**MY PAIN POINTS, PROBLEMS, AND ISSUES LED UP TO MY TRANSFORMATIONAL JOURNEY DURING COLLEGE**</u>

College life wasn't the remedy for my problem, and I was once proud to participate in a nationwide statistic when Stillwater, OK, was the #1 City in America in beer consumption. I certainly did drink my fair share of beer to help the numbers. At the end of my 2nd semester, I got so drunk at a party that my dear teammates placed me spread eagle on top of a car. They each held one of my limbs while taking me back to my dorm, Iba Hall. Silly things happen after drinking too much.

One night, I had a brush with the law when I was too wasted to drive my car. My buddy, Heat, was the designated driver when the police pulled us over. We got out of the car, and he presented insurance verification. I stood there with my hands behind my back because I knew how this was going to end. I had an open container of beer, a bottle of whiskey, an ounce of weed, and a gram of cocaine under the driver's seat. I stood there praying while my heart was racing. A million thoughts were going through my head, wondering how my parents would respond to me on the phone. Fortunately enough, I never had to make that call. After the officers checked our identifications, we were free to go. One officer said angrily, "You need to get your tag light fixed before driving at night in this town!" I was more than thankful that that was the only problem.

In another situation, after making another fool of myself one night in Columbus, OH, I hugged a street light pole to stand up. I knew this irrational behavior had to end. I was so wasted that the strangers passing by made comments like 'Your girlfriend sure is skinny' and 'Stop squeezing your girl so hard, you're making her change colors.' I was in survival mode, and it wasn't funny to me then. I realized then that this wasn't how I wanted to live the rest of my life, just sipping on a bottle. I needed an immediate transformation. The Almighty God stepped in, and I haven't drunk that much alcohol since my following prayer, "Please get me back to the hotel. I won't do it again." That's a promise that I've kept. My transformational change led me to my spiritual awakening, the wind beneath my wings of change.

MY SPIRITUAL AWAKENING

At age 24, I was introduced to books that positively influenced me and my research on Positive Mental Attitude. I learned that I could change the course of my life by controlling my thoughts and the words that came out of my mouth. Prov. 18:21 says: "Death and Life are in the power of the tongue. And they that love it will eat its fruit." The words settled in, and I realized that I had the power to generate the positives or negatives in my life. This was a big-time game-changer for me.

This was during my time in the DMV (Washington, D.C., Maryland, Virginia) area while working with the Charles O. Scott organization, a sales team of highly motivated, melanated people with goals for a better life. We had a mandatory book reading list, which was the most extraordinary discipline imposed upon me. I grew as a man by following the advice of others who walked before sharing their ups and downs of becoming successful. The authors included Earl Nightingale, Zig Ziglar, Og Mandino, David Schwartz, and Dale Carnegie. I continued reading self-help books and listening to many speakers who encouraged me that I could do whatever I set my mind to. Today, I am still building on that foundation so I can help others.

While in the DMV area, I visited the King Library frequently to continue studying the great leader of the Civil Rights Movement, where I learned about his past, which was like mine. He also played with white kids in his neighborhood until they reached a certain age. The parents of less melanated children would draw a line of division. No more playing with 'them.' Dr. King also grew up in church, learning the doctrinally correct teachings of his time. He knew it was not fair for Black citizens to be treated as animals. Little by little, he made progress with the help of multiple organizations. For the record, while Dr. King was as peaceful as history paints him, another side was buried by our government for 50 years.

White America didn't want his aggressive side to be known, so we only got to learn about the peaceful side of Dr. King. He wrote a sermon before he was assassinated, titled, 'Why America May Go to Hell,' which was part of the artifacts from room 316 in the Lorraine Hotel in Memphis, Tennessee. Dr. King was not killed because he was nice and peaceful. He was gunned down because he was a leader who was exposing American wrongs to the American people. Food for thought: Why were his personal belongings kept from the public for 50 years? He was carrying a torch for Black America, for equality and civil rights. Many laws were changed with the efforts of those who led the struggle. Once Dr. King was killed, the Civil Rights Movement was never the same.

My life has had many significant periods that include losing multiple close friends before turning the age of 21 and being away from family and friends while living on the East Coast. My first marriage ended in divorce, and my career served as a teacher, administrator, and especially as a grandparent. All of these things made this life of mine interesting. A person recently referred to me as a Renaissance man, and I accept that title wholeheartedly.

MY CAREER AND COMMUNITY SERVICE

After a couple of stops in Dallas, Texas, and Washington, DC, I settled in my hometown, where we raised a family, bought a house, and served in my church and community at multiple levels. As a career educator, I have enjoyed serving numerous school districts and countless students from diverse backgrounds. In addition, I served as an on-field football official for over twenty years, including high school, college, and lower levels of professional experience.

To improve, I organized officiating camps to understand the game better, and officials from the NFL and Big 12 would conduct the training. Many regional officials would attend, and we would develop lifelong friendships in this fraternity. Many of these guys are seen on Saturdays and Sundays still doing their 'thang' today on nationally televised games.

My wife, Liz, and I raised a successful blended family with systems, policies, and procedures to keep order in our house. I like to refer to it as a 'scientific experiment' because I closely monitored every aspect of the family. Discipline was the key to all the working parts, and no one had too big of a responsibility. Everyone doing their part was enough to keep the house in proper working order. The make-up of the family included mine, yours, and ours. Consistency as parents made our household successful. Looking back, the most important thing I ever did to direct our family was creating the 'No Touching Policy,' which my grown kids scoff at today. It kept the peace most of the time. I expected everyone to always keep their hands to themselves, eliminating most confusion.

THE EPIPHANY AND TRANSFORMATION

While flying over the Atlantic Ocean and returning from a visit to Germany, an epiphany occurred to me. I've never been able to shake loose since that moment. While in Vecta, Germany, I could hang my coat on a wall while I watched my nephew play a professional basketball game. When I returned afterward, it was still there. I thought about that moment, "What kind of country (USA) do I live in? Why isn't this our norm?" Wow!! My coat wasn't touched by anyone else! While walking through the marketplaces, I noticed most people's expressions and would nod at a few to get a response from time to time.

I realized after seeing hundreds of people there weren't any hateful American eyes looking at me. What a shock that was to me. So, when I was on the plane thinking about the people from Germany, I created a plan to handle this new revelation after all the years of 'hateful eyes' being my norm. It took prayer and intentionality to move forward, and forgiveness became the kryptonite I used to attack it. Luke 6:38 says,".... forgive, and you will be forgiven." Matt 18:22 says we are to forgive those who sin against us 490 times/day for each person. That sounds impossible, but my wife, who hits 485 almost daily, has challenged me. I'm just kidding, but you get my point. I must have a forgiving heart to live successfully in this brainwashed society. That's my choice, and I make lemonade with what I'm working with.

MY SPIRITUAL GUIDANCE AND LISTENING THE HOLY SPIRIT

I bought a book in 2020 titled 'Dangerous Prayers' by Craig Groeschel; for most, it is a simple two-hour read. I don't fit that category, so it took me longer. The book contains three dangerous prayers,

1. Search Me.
2. Break Me.
3. Send Me.

The summary asked, "If you could pray a 4th Dangerous Prayer, what would it be?" I immediately prayed, 'Lord, do something through me that is so big that the whole world will know it is you and not me.' Simple, right? A few weeks later, on Pentecost Sunday, May 31, 2020, I worked out the mission statement to 'Unite Black America, financially.' Over the past 3 ½ years, I've received the details to complete this mission, but not without many miscalculations, mistakes, breakups, and countless disappointments.

I've also met a new group of friends who share a similar vision to unite Black America and return to the days of Black Wall Street when we supported each other in business, civic groups, neighborhoods, and everything our ancestors set out to do. There was always unified support.

The one person who kept the fire under my feet was Vee from California, who would periodically call and say, 'When are we getting Black Wall Street started? I want to be part of this.' She began introducing me to members of a Mastermind Group who helped organize the Million Man March in Washington, D.C. The members included business owners, one manuscript coach, truck drivers, health and wellness experts, and many other occupations. These people were influential in my development, and they were willing to share their experiences to assist me in my mission.

All this came together after the Holy Spirit caught my attention, and I've been paying close attention as though my life depended on it. It all depends on me being obedient and serving others.

I've learned a few things about my Comforter (Holy Spirit) during my transformation:

> He counsels me.
> He teaches me.
> He guides me.

He taught me to listen to His still, quiet voice and remain ready at any moment. When I hear the Master's voice, I respond because I've decided to obey His voice. John 10:4 says, 'And when he puts forth his own sheep, he goes before them, and the sheep follow him: for they know his voice.' I had to learn to listen when counseled by unexpected people the Almighty was using to get my attention. It all happens for a purpose and is a part of the process I had to go through to reach this point. I know (for sure) that I don't look like what I've been through. Praise God!

You don't have to get ready when you stay ready! That's what a close relationship with the Almighty is all about—knowing Him, knowing His voice! Jeffery Satinover said, "I have often wondered why the voice of God is so quiet and so still. Perhaps He is trying to train us to listen. Just as by His very quiet, the gentlemen in a room full of shouting oafs (eventually) compels attention. Perhaps God draws us to His voice not by outshouting our inner babble, but by the whispered truths that reveal His character." I have also heard it said: "The practice of listening is crucial to posturing a man for everything his heart will need to receive. Asking and inviting God to speak, then listening…this is the practice of an oriented man, the practice of a Warrior Heart."

Learning to listen is a process I had to go through to understand my Why, allowing me to experience the answer to my Dangerous Prayer. My heart is so set on unifying Black America that it drives me daily to reach further for the solution to bring us all together as a Nation of people, living peacefully with each other.

The Holy Spirit guides me to be in the right places at the right times. You know how that feels, right? Commuting to work provides quite a bit of time to pray and listen to the encouraging words of Joel Osteen or Craig Groeschel. Hearing is a physical thing that we do with our ears. However, the Holy Spirit speaks to our hearts, minds, and souls with resounding, penetrating thoughts beyond my normal. This is what guides me.

For example, I've been trying to reach a particular person for a follow-up conversation as instructed, but none of the methods I used to contact him worked. After six months of trying to connect with him, I sat behind him at an event honoring a mutual friend, and we connected at that point. It wasn't a coincidence that I took off work that day, drove across the state to be there, and had an open seat directly behind him. I credit my listening skills, not hearing, to this heavenly moment.

Joel Osteen teaches about having a close relationship with the Creator of the Universe. He brags about how the Almighty blesses him, his family, the ministry, and everything that he puts his hands on, and that renews my spirit to get to know Him more. Craig Groeschel tells about his sinful past and how his relationship with God is restored because of his admissions for his wrongdoing.

Even while driving, the Comforter tells me when to change lanes and when there is an issue in front of me, always keeping me prepared for the obstacles on the road and for unsafe drivers. He guides me through the pages of the Bible to read specific scriptures to prepare my heart for what I will encounter in the future. I depend on this Holy guidance with all my heart, so I listen, not just hear.

Have you ever noticed the sound (ear) in the middle of the word heart? The heart can hear; the Holy Spirit speaks to my heart through my ears. I love the song, 'Goodness of God'. It is beautiful to me, and it doesn't matter who sings the words. Recently, I re-read the lyrics to the song and discovered a deeper meaning. My heart had attached itself to the music because that's my story.

My transformation is rooted in listening to (hearing) the voice of the Creator of the Universe and responding to His call. I prayed for the ability to use more of my brain, 2% more than average, and knowledge has poured into me like never before. I can solve problems faster than before, and applied wisdom is always close by. I read daily affirmations to remind me what the Word says about me and who I am. Kenneth Copeland provided this statement, and I have personalized it and repeated it for over 20 years:

WHO DO YOU THINK YOU ARE? I'M GLAD THAT YOU ASKED THAT

I'm a child of the Most High God!
I'm a King's kid!
I'm blessed going in!
I'm blessed going out!
I'm blessed in the City!
I'm blessed in the Field!
I'm the head, not the tail!
I'm above only, not beneath!
I'm the lender and not the borrower!
I'm the righteousness of God!
I'm more than a Conqueror!
I'm Healed!
I'm Delivered!
I'm faithful!
I'm Prosperous!
I'm the redeemed of the Lord!
I'm Victorious!
I'm a follower of the Holy Ghost!
I'm under the shadow of the Almighty!
I'm followed by Mercy and Grace!
I'm an Overcomer!
I'm Fruitful!
I'm a believer!
I'm a distribution center!
I'm a Whosoever!

<u>AS TIMMY THINKS IN HIS HEART, SO IS HE!</u>

I have spoken positive words throughout my life and gladly receive positive words from others, but my spirit responds exceptionally well when it's from me.

I loved the quote from Creflo Dollar Jr. when he was addressing criticism he received from the media regarding his pursuit of a new airplane:

"Can't nobody tell me what I can believe my God for!" I feel the same way. Get out of my Kool-aid and make your own. I believe in the Word of God. I believe I can have what it says, and I can do what it says I can do. I trust the Almighty God!

<u>MY FUTURE PROJECT</u>

My next project is "Brainwashed to Whitewash," The Unconscious Shaping of the American Mind. In this book, I'll share my life experiences, the repetitive messages and images that drew me to the television, and how they shaped my thinking. This book will hold your attention, educate you, and make you look in the mirror.

ABOUT THE AUTHOR

TIMOTHY D. YOUNG, M.Ed

Timothy D. Young, M.Ed., is a multifaceted individual whose passion for education, entrepreneurship, and community empowerment has profoundly driven him to impact various spheres of society. Born and raised in Shawnee, Oklahoma, Young has dedicated his life to serving others and effecting positive change within his community.

Young's journey in education spans an impressive 27 years, during which he has held diverse roles, including Teacher's Assistant, Teacher, Coach, Assistant Principal, Athletic Director, and Principal. His commitment to nurturing young minds and fostering academic excellence has earned him widespread admiration and respect among students, colleagues, and parents.

Beyond his contributions to the Field of Education, Young's visionary leadership extends to his roles as an entrepreneur and community activist. Recognizing the importance of unity and collaboration, he founded the Black Wall Street Private Group to unify Black America financially through cooperative efforts within Black American communities. Young seeks to empower individuals and businesses through this initiative, leveraging their collective strength to achieve greater political and economic influence.

As a community activist, Young has been instrumental in addressing various issues facing Shawnee, Oklahoma, and beyond. His collaborative approach, working closely with community members and as a director on numerous boards, including the City Council of Shawnee, reflects his dedication to finding innovative solutions and creating positive change.

Young's academic credentials include a master's in education administration from East Central University in Ada, Oklahoma, a bachelor's in criminal justice, and a minor in Military Science. His academic background and extensive practical experience have equipped him with the knowledge and skills necessary to excel in his various roles as an educator, leader, and advocate.

Outside of his professional pursuits, Timmy finds joy in spending time with his family, including his wife Liz, their five children, and five grandchildren. He cherishes moments of togetherness and finds relaxation in baking, golfing, fishing, and participating in cultural festivals and reunions.

Timothy D. Young, M.Ed., remains deeply committed to (his mission of) fostering education, entrepreneurship, and community empowerment. Through his unwavering dedication and visionary leadership, he inspires and uplifts those around him, leaving a lasting legacy of positive impact and meaningful change.

Email: timmy.young@sbcglobal.net
Instagram: @ibtyubu
Linkedin: Timmy Young
Messenger: Timmy Young

CHAPTER TWELVE
THE MIND WITH TOGETHERNESS, HISTORICALLY, TAKES YOU WHERE YOUR TALENTS ALONE CAN'T
DR. JOESEPH WEBB III (USA)

Growing up on the East Side of Cleveland, Ohio, was not bad as a kid, but it did have its challenges. No, we did not have to worry about food on the table. Still, I had surrounding family members and homeys who had to hustle on a daily to provide for themselves: collecting pop bottles, stuffing mailboxes, delivering papers, bagging groceries, shoveling snow, washing cars, and performing simple, handy tasks for our seniors; like going to the store or taking out their garbage cans. Some of my homeys did it to survive. I did it to make some extra money. Between that weekly allowance I got from my Dad and these hustle options, I always kept a little money in my pocket. As I got older, some hustles evolved into more questionable activities. To protect the innocent and those associated, I will leave that out of the context of this story.

My Dad, Joseph Webb Jr, was a hardworking man, a businessman, and a hustler! My Dad did what it took to 'HAVE MORE' for himself, his family, and anyone who rolled with him. My Dad worked as an Auto Inspector at the General Motors/Chevrolet Plant in Parma, Ohio. My Dad, Joseph Jr, owned a General Store and had other business involvements that I will leave out of the context of this story. May Joseph Webb Jr. rest in peace. My Dad's accomplishments in post-Jim Crow Law and The Civil Rights movement era were phenomenal. However, the struggle of running a business while working 40 PLUS hours a week and dealing with the haters of so-called family and friends would be the demise of our General Store. Despite that, the entrepreneurial seed that I have today was planted. Thank You, Dad! I am just a microcosm of history and how profound it has been over the last 400 PLUS years. *Once we know better, we do better.* We need to learn from the greatness of our past and modify our beliefs in what greatness is, especially as people of color. Get ready to learn!

From Bondage to Bondage, we have gone full circle. From shackles to fat gold chains. From physical bondage to bondage of the mind. From dying by the chains being wrapped around our necks, ankles, and wrists to dying for wanting those fat gold chains around our necks, ankles, and wrists. What an Oxymoron! Although they both show opposite examples of slavery (Physical vs Mental), one depicts stolen identity and the other lost identity.

After the unfortunate national public murder of Mr. George Floyd that went viral in 2020, "The Woke Period" for our Gen Y & Gen Zers of all races was a good thing. However, it revealed our Children's lost identity crisis. I watched a college football game on national television, and the cameras showed a young black athlete wearing a t-shirt that said "Chains, Tattoos, Dreads, and WE ARE." As much as I understood the point that he was attempting to make, we are so much more than that. The depth of us as a people is just as profound as the depth of the bondage that has scarred us.

Bondage, by definition, is the state of being a slave, controlled. There are many types of bondage. Physical bondage is the state of being physically controlled or bound in shackles, chains, or jail cells, for example. Mental bondage is the most powerful type of bondage. The shackles are around the mind. It is a subconscious phenomenon that controls the mindset through what we watch and listen to.

Cell phones, video games, television, radio, and social media are nothing to be played with and must be done in moderation, or they will take you out like they almost took me out. I was a part of the video game fad with Nintendo, Atari, Galaga, Asteroids, Space Invaders, Centipede & Pac Man, and I WAS THE MAN! My hip-hop days went into the Gangsta Rap Era as it was getting started, and guess what? I was getting started as a Gangsta in college in my Tricked-out Bonneville with the Trues & Twos (Rims & Tires). These things were major distractors. Had it not been for my mother, Jannarosa Webb, who opened my mail to read my winter semester failing report card during my sophomore year of college, my distractions would have gotten me kicked out. Thank

You, Mom. It was a wake-up call to self-pride, dignity, and WANTING MORE out of life.

Getting out of my community and joining the Military to see the world did not prevent me from experiencing some of the challenges of Racism, Divorce, and Financial Bondage in my own life as an adult and, in my family circles, the struggles of drugs. The sudden death of my father while I was in High School derailed our family life train. The allowances were gone, and we were sinking fast financially to the lower class, so we had to get odd-end jobs to help our Mom, who now worked two jobs, make things happen.

I also tapped into the underground world of hustling, which included working with "Chop Shops" and brokering Auto Parts to junkyards and My Homey's, who "Placed Special Orders" for cassette players, stereo systems, tires, plush car seats; *anything you needed, I was able, and if I didn't have it, I had connections.* It was all about the Benjamin's Baby! Status, competition, and "The Ladies is what we called them." All of this continued after I made it through high school, went to college locally, and worked at a bakery in the mid-shift.

I was hustling and making good money but was wearing down and going nowhere fast. I thank God for a hardworking, loving, and wise mother who saw what was going on, "opened" my college report card my sophomore year and gave me the "*What the Hell are you doing!*" speech.

I had to join the Air Force to get away! Reflecting on these mental, physical, and emotional challenges as a young adult and even today has allowed me to look through a different lens to repair any damage and refrain from causing any further damage. Thank God for wisdom! The Air Force pulled me out of that sinking, distracted, lost hole going nowhere. My loving mother and the Military saved my life.

Emotional bondage tears down our communities, families, and ourselves. How will you ever love your neighbor if you don't love yourself? How could you be your Brother's Keeper? The Good Book says to *"Love thy neighbor."* Spiritual bondage ties into how we make decisions, right versus wrong, moral versus immoral, and good versus bad. Then, there's material bondage. This is the core of our financial crisis, the "Gotta have it now," microwave, instant gratification society. Modern-day idolatry KILLS. Listen, it's okay to have nice things, just don't let nice things have you! Slavery, even to nice things, is dangerous.

Speaking of dangerous situations, historically, it started for us when the first enslaved Africans touched American soil in the mid-1500s to begin our 400-plus years of slavery. Yes, I'm sure you're saying, "I already knew that," but did you know that in the 1700s, one of our most popular urban cities, New York, was one the only cities in the north that was a proponent of slavery? Our New York Stock Exchange was born. Can you guess who was being sold as stock? We (Black people) were! Or shall I say enslaved people, depending on who reads this book? During my internet research, I came across this comment: *"Initially, buying and selling slaves was done privately. Then the New York City Council declared that all Negro and Indian Slaves that were let out of prison would be hired at the Market House at the Wall Street Slip because of anxiety and fear coming from the White Middle Class."*

New York, New York, big city of dreams, but everything in New York ain't always what it seems! The irony is, although we were the "first stock" sold on the New York Stock Exchange, this despicable act placed a higher value on us per se than we figuratively place on ourselves and each other today…. **We are Whole, Perfect, Strong, Powerful, Loving, Harmonious, and Happy! Let's go deeper…So we fought…**

The American Civil War was fought in The United States from 1861-1865 after a longstanding controversy over slavery. United States President Abraham Lincoln issued The Emancipation Proclamation on January 1st, 1863. Are you ready for the irony? The American Revolutionary War was fought in The United States from 1775-1783. George Washington led the troops to freedom for America with The Declaration of Independence on July 4th, 1776. Talk about skewed identity bondage! "We, the people," who (literally) built this country called The United States of America, who fought for its freedom, were not included in the 4th of July celebration. We had to fight our own War 90 years later for freedom in the country that was built on our backs! The fight continues. The history books praise George Washington (slave owner) and his efforts to free America on July 4[th,] Independence Day, 1776, yet speak very little about Abraham Lincoln's efforts to free The Black Slaves, with The Emancipation Proclamation and Juneteenth, June 19th, 1865. We must remember the fight from which we came to know the shoulders on which we stood.

These create the path to where we should go and where we ought to be. My time in the Military gave me a deeper understanding of United States History and our role in it.

Understanding The National and Global Mission of what allows us to sleep at night and go anywhere we want is priceless. I got into business with my Air Force Brothers and purchased my first Real Estate Investment Property while in the Air Force. The Air Force took me from the confines of my Black Afrocentric Community, where I was amongst a majority, to the world of mainstream, where, for the first time, I learned what it meant to be a minority in America. The Air Force averaged, in my eyes, about 10 Blacks for every 100 Whites in any given Military Unit. It was even less when I traveled overseas to Air Force Bases in other countries.

My success and challenges in The Air Force prepared me for the challenges of Mainstream America, which is still a journey to this day. If we, as Black Afro-Americans, only knew what we had done for Mainstream America, including the Industrial Revolution, we would have so much to be proud of.

Here are just a few of our Black contributions to The Industrial Revolution.

Granville T. Woods – *1901- Inventor of The Rail Electrical Switching Systems. Mr. Woods made Mr. Vandrbilt's Railroad better!*
Garret Morgan – *1923- Traffic Light. The Traffic Light today prevents chaos on our roads and has saved millions of lives.*

Dr. Daniel Hale Williams – 1893 – *Performed the first successful open-heart surgery in the United States.*
Dr. Charles Drew – 1939 – *Developed novel methods for storing blood plasma (The Red Cross).*
John Stoddard – 1899- *Invented the Ice Box.*
Fredrick M. Jones – 1949- *Invented the Refrigeration System (Air Conditioning).*
Madam CJ Walker – 1908 – *Opened Beauty School (First Black woman millionaire in America).*
Dr. George F. Grant – 1910- *Invented the Golf Tee. Need I say more?*

Our Black successes and creativity allowed us at one time in history to thrive in our own Black Towns known as Black Wall Street. There were more than 60 "Black Wall Streets" in the United States, which Norman L. Corbett wrote about in his book "The Black Towns." "The Black Towns" is a must-have for your library. The largest and most famous of the "Black Wall Streets" was The Greenwood District of Tulsa, Oklahoma. As the former Director for Black Wall Street USA's Economic Development Council, I participated in the 100th (Year) Recognition Anniversary of the destruction of Tulsa's Greenwood District. The Greenwood District existed from 1905 to 1921 with over 600 Black-owned Businesses. The city was so wealthy that if Tulsa, Oklahoma Greenwood District existed today, it would be a producing city of $280 billion a year. The mighty dollar circulated through our Black communities back then for up to 13 MONTHS. That is four times more than the dollar circulation for today's Asians, Jewish, Whites, and Hispanics combined. Unfortunately for us today, the dollar does not even last a workday in our communities. Only Six Hours!

The visit to Tulsa was very enlightening yet bittersweet. It was great to hear about a city that once thrived with 40 blocks of Black Enterprise Ownership, now a fraction of itself, down to two city blocks and very little ownership. My tenure as The BWSUSA EDC Director taught me that these issues are not isolated.

As I communicated with the various Black Wall Street USA State Directors, I learned that different states faced the same issues. The same story played out in the community I grew up in: the East Side of Cleveland - Glenville Ward. When I was a child and until I left the city for The Air Force in 1985, Blacks owned the Grocery Stores, The Auto Shops, The Cleaners, The Restaurants, etc. You name it, we owned it until the drugs took over the city and gentrification started to show up. The passing of Civil Rights Bills of the '60s, which included Voting Rights and Fair Housing Acts, were supposed to have even more impact on the former and prevent the latter.

Looking at things through today's lenses, two generations later, are those same laws benefiting us today? Are we empowered or enabled today? Our last 50-plus years have been critical. We have gone from being independent-minded and wanting our own to being dependent and wanting free cheese from the Government. This dependency has enabled us through government programs. We have not "faired well" with The Welfare System. We have become Projects in the Hood. Our neighborhoods are looking like Third World Countries with no fight, purpose, or crusade but to destroy one another. An idle mind is truly the devil's playground. Because of my Dad and the community I grew up in, I did experience the benefits of the Civil Rights Era Acts. My Dad, our neighbors, and many of my older extended family members were employed at institutions that put us in middle-class status. Some of these institutions were GM Chevrolet, Ford Mercury, Lincoln Electric, The Illuminating Company, LTV Steel, and many local Government Careers.

Our family benefited from the Civil Rights Era of the 60s. Our middle-class status allowed us to move on to homeownership when I was six. My sister, Jakeba, was able to attend private school and never saw a Public School classroom a day in her life. My brothers, Jamez and Javarre, and I never had to wear hand-me-downs from anyone or shop at the Goodwill. The Civil Rights Era Acts were a "Great Start" for their time period, but they do not hold the accountable strength to deal with today's Fair Housing Act challenges, education disparities, voter suppression, and wealth inequality. The Welfare System has crippled us to the point where it is not uncommon to see three generations of a family on food stamps and living in Section 8 Project Housing at home, watching mindless television all day, waiting for those monthly funds to come in from the Government.

The U.S. Air Force prevented me from having those experiences. It gave me the training needed to keep up with the latest technology. The Military GI Bill allowed me to finish college with a Bachelor's Degree in Non-Profit Business Administration and a Master's in Biblical Studies. I fulfilled a 30-year career in the Military and retired with an Honorable Discharge! Hoorah! Many doors of opportunity opened for me. I enjoyed a career in the energy sector, invested in residential real estate, and eventually transitioned to full-time entrepreneurship in financial services and business development.

Dr. Martin Luther King Jr. did play a significant role in my parents' lives as well the lives of many other Americans when it came to the idea of "Equality." However, the other "E word" missing in his messages was "Economics." The I Have a Dream" speech (1963) focused on a colorless, harmonic society working together for the greater good, righteous and noble. Dr. King's last most powerful speech, "I've Been to the Mountaintop" (1968), emphasized economic growth, our consumerism curse, and the almighty dollar. April 3rd was the speech; April 4th was the assassination. Imagine how different our lives would have been had we gotten the total message of Dr. Martin Luther King's vision.

"It is a cruel fact that the Negro, generally speaking, has not developed a responsible sense of financial values. The best economist says that our automobile should not cost more than half your annual income, but we see many Negroes earning $7,000/year paying for a $5,000 car. The home, it is said, should not cost more than twice the annual income, but we see many Negroes earning $8,000/year living in a $30,000 house."

This excerpt came from an article interview with Dr. King from Playboy Magazine, JAN 1965. In 1965, we were only 11% of the population, yet we consumed 40% of the Whiskey (Alcohol) in the United States. In 1965, we spent over 72 Million Dollars annually in the jewelry stores! Today, we spend over $385 Million a year. With the fat gold chain phenomenon, I'm surprised it's not more. We missed the memo! This lifeline would have changed our trajectory. Instead of wealth and equality, we got integration, consumerism, and gentrification.

Integration is the intermixing of people or groups previously segregated. *Integration without reciprocation equals no dollar circulation.* Our focus was "The moving on up thing" to the east side, the heights, or the suburbs. For some reason, it meant that you arrived to be amongst people who wanted nothing to do with you at that time. That "Moving on up" thing depleted the Black community of its resources, talent, revenue, and most importantly, Love. The Black community has become a Third World Country with broken families, gang violence, drive-by shootings, drugs, and baby-mama-with-daddy drama. The deadly spirit of inequality has risen its ugly head in our communities amongst ourselves!

Equality is the state of being equal, especially in status, rights, and opportunities. The spirit of inequality in our communities is different but not much different. We started putting statuses on one another. We started putting each other down and not "keeping" one another. We started bullying, hating, and killing one another. Economically, we stopped supporting one another's businesses. Add to "System Racism" the fact that the racists know we're committing genocide by cannibalizing one another. I call it covert slavery. Some believe we are still slaves.

Here's what they are saying. *They (the racists) will continue to reap profits from us without shackles by using ignorance as a primary weapon of containment. Greed is another weapon of containment. THEY SAY that we'd rather buy new sneakers, name-brand shoes, new cars, nails, and hair than invest in a business or a home. We (as Blacks) will continue to show off to one another with material things while THEY benefit from our spending. Our selfishness does not allow us to be able to work together on any project of substance.* **We must break this poverty chain...**

Consumerism is society's preoccupation with the acquisition of consumer goods. This materialistic "gotta have it now" mindset places us as a people in the number one spot of consumerism. We spend more than 1.2 Trillion dollars annually in the U.S. economy.

That is more than the domestic product of 80 countries worldwide. So, we do have money as a people, but it's in the wrong places! I believe and have proven that trust with applied Group Economics can help take us from the consuming to the producing mentality. This could position us to revitalize communities (ourselves) by taking on gentrification as an opportunity instead of looking at it as some curse or conspiracy.

Gentrification is renovating deteriorated urban neighborhoods (Not Communities) through the influx of more affluent residents. This is a common and controversial topic in politics and urban planning. Gentrification can improve the quality of a neighborhood. It can also potentially force relocation of current, established residents and businesses, causing them to move from a gentrified area seeking lower-cost housing and stores.

Gentrification is a business that we, unfortunately, are entirely on the wrong side of. We depreciate the property value of our neighborhoods by destroying them and making them unsafe even for us to live in. This "Urban Jungle" creates the opportunity for others to come in and purchase our properties for pennies on the dollar. This happened in Cleveland, Ohio, and Miami, Florida.

My hometown, Cleveland, has a dynamic where the Whites are moving from the Suburbs back to Clevland's inner City, East Side, West Side, and Downtown areas. My travels have seen gentrification thriving in Atlanta, Georgia, Los Angeles, California's Urban areas (Compton, Englewood), Detroit, Michigan, and New York (Harlem, Brooklyn, Queens, etc.). To all of these Local governments' chagrin, they are simply trying to generate revenue for their townships and counties; It's a business decision. We must be about each other's business and working together (on purpose) for a purpose.

The Military taught me firsthand how we were never alone in anything we did; if one person failed, we all failed. No one went home if all mission-oriented duties were not done at the end of the day. If the Fighter Jets were not prepped and mission-ready (Especially Overseas), then NO ONE LEFT the base. I also saw this in the communities where I lived and worked as a civilian and a business owner. While in the Air Force, stationed in Suwon,

South Korea, (1988) (Summer Olympics), I got my first dose of watching the Korean culture work together and help each other in the business districts of the Korean Cities. Even in competition, if they did not have what you needed or could not create what you wanted to have made (very talented people), they would (literally) walk you down the street to the vendor who had it or who could.

In Miami, you see the same dynamic with Hispanics helping one another fulfill the American Dream of homeownership. We used to joke about how two or three families with six cars out front would pile into a house living together. But it was to help each other purchase a home for each family successfully. Our Black-divided neighborhoods are now becoming their family-oriented communities. Who's laughing now? My experience with the Jewish culture has been the same. I experienced this in Finance while working at a majority Jewish Financial Firm. The Jewish are very nice people that would help anytime you "asked" for their assistance. They would also help you with anything that produced results.

In my experience, however, you had to ask. When it came to the Jewish working amongst themselves, they were a tight community that showed each other all the ropes, not just the ones you asked about. That used to burn me up, especially when they would send all the new Black hires to me for mentorship. They mentored "their own," and even those Jewish Agents who came after me thrived. I later learned to appreciate what was happening and realized it was cultural. I did say that my Jewish Colleagues would assist when asked.

My desire intensified to seek the building of a Black Community that didn't believe in scarcity but believed that "together everyone achieves more" (TEAM) and that "Teamwork makes the Dream work." As such, I co-founded the Black Wealth Consortium – mission: To revitalize Black communities by leveraging asset collecting to foster generational wealth building. We must change our bondage mindset. To break the chains of bondage, we must come together and commune. We must be about each other's business, not just for ourselves, not just for our people, but for everyone. You are not going to become successful being a Super Hero in a neighborhood silo.

My Dad was a Super-Hero in a siloed situation. A lot of our communities are dangerously siloed. This keeps us out of the mainstream and into Third World lifestyles. My successes have come through melting pot opportunities and the ability to work with everyone. My World Renowned Mentor and Colleague, Dr. George C. Fraser, says, "We, as Black People, have everything we need to be successful...Except ourselves!" It is time to get off the hamster wheel of bondage.

Let us release (Not forget) the horrors of the past and embrace our richness. We have done great things, for we are whole, NOT THREE FIFTHS! We are perfect in God's image and have achieved miraculous levels, unthinkable achievements from the Pyramids to outer space. We are strong, resilient people who know how to love but have lost some of that loving feeling. Start with LOVING YOURSELF.

You are great! Let us commune in harmony and get rid of the internal "Jim Crow" mess that keeps us down like crabs in a bucket. I know that when we know better, we do better. Let's do better together. PEACE!

ABOUT THE AUTHOR

DR. JOSEPH WEBB III, CRFA, CLTC

Dr. Joseph Webb III maintains a serious commitment to his clients. Joe helps his clients reach the next level of financial success through seminars, financial counseling, debt relief, and comprehensive financial planning. Joe and the financial professionals at Profit Planners MGA, LLC provide investment services, asset protection, tax strategies, specialized insurance, and survivor assistance.

Along with his role at Profit Planners MGA, LLC, Joe also helps small business decision-makers discover innovative tax-saving and expense-reducing solutions to increase the company's bottom line. He does this without reducing the quality of service and at no financial risk. He also works with different churches and their conventions, holding workshops on financial literacy. He was appointed Financial Secretary/Treasurer for the Baptist Ministers Council of South Florida. He is also the COO of the South Dade Chamber of Commerce. Dr. Webb is also involved with the United Nations as a "Peace Ambassador for the Bahamas."

Dr. Webb received his education through Kaplan Financial University and St. Thomas Christian University. He has also served his country in the Air Force Reserves for over 30 years. He is married with three children and three grandchildren.

Profit Planners MGA, LLC

8925 SW 148th St., Suite 200 – Palmetto ay, FL 33176

Phone: (305) 969 –3644 - Fax: (305) 964-5724
Website: www.profitplannersmg.com
Email: joewebb@profitplannersmg.com
LinkedIn: Profitplannersmg@gmail.com
Instagram: contactprofitplanners@gmail.com

CHAPTER THIRTEEN
DRIVEN BY PURPOSE
RAYSHUN SCOTT (USA)

To fully grasp every aspect of life, you must see good, evil, the beautiful, and the ugly, the Yin and the Yang. If you were always happy, would you appreciate hearing good news? Would you be joyous whenever an accomplishment was achieved from a goal that you set? Would life seem worth it? The same applies if you lived the opposite way and were always sad.

When we go through our trials and tribulations, our better times are cherished. They are sometimes the only thing that keeps us going. Those memories of laughter, love, and life can be among the most powerful "weapons" in our arsenal for overcoming tough times. Going to our first sports game, taking a vacation for the first time, your family greeting you at the door when you arrive home, etc. All these examples are memories that help keep a smile on our faces. Without the sadness, we couldn't experience joy.

All these things that I've stated are realizations and epiphanies I've personally experienced throughout my years of life. We've all had our moments of ups and downs. Some of those downs felt like they never had a bottom and that it would last forever. The hardest thing about experiencing those painful, soul-crushing moments is realizing an ugly truth. The ugly truth is that even though you're going through one (or some) of the most challenging times of your life, the world doesn't stop moving on your account. Your loved ones still need your attention. Your job/career still requires you to fulfill your duties. GOD (or whatever you call your Higher Power) still has work for you to do.

We often go into a perplexing system of ifs, ands, whats, buts. Why? Because, quite frankly, sometimes we don't know the answers. We don't know the who, what, why, when, or how when we are trying to figure things out, and by things, I mean OURSELVES. That's mainly what it all boils down to when we enter this stage of our lives. This stage of our lives is called growth, which can be very painful. Comfortability eliminates our dreams, so there is beauty in the ugly, just as there is ugly in the beauty.

After reading these passages, you may have realized that we ALL go through life with our share of happiness and sadness, war and peace, hate and love, etc. My story may sound similar, if not the same, to most or unrelatable to others. Either way, it's my story, and I am sharing it hoping it will do these two things. It shows that there is always a light at the end of the tunnel, and leaning on GOD (or whatever you call your Higher Power) will help you get through it all.

As mentioned in my bio, I worked at a company for nearly ten years. When I first started there, I had no clue that my experiences there would be a key to molding me into who I am now. Remember, everyone, we learn and grow daily, so don't ever think you're at your peak. I came in as a regular employee just trying to make money to take care of myself and my responsibilities. I had a daughter and another baby on the way. I was out of a job for about four months and was falling behind on my bills. I had no plan but to bring in income.

Time went on, and I was continually learning the ins and outs of the company. I was informed that I had the potential to move up the corporate ladder. I interviewed and became a supervisor. I was joyous as I had the opportunity to demonstrate my growing leadership capabilities and increase my income. Everything was going well, and I was a rising star. I was bestowed wisdom from many sources, and one of the things I know is that the higher you climb, the more turbulent your climb becomes.

One day, my team assisted me with unloading trailers and bringing merchandise back into the facility. One of my crewmates had an important call regarding his family, and I excused him from his duties. One of my managers was looking from afar and noticed that he (my crewmate) wasn't working and was on the phone. All my manager saw was the supervisor working harder than his crew. Eventually, my crewmate got back to work so we could finish our tasks. I was summoned into a meeting with my manager, and what he said shocked me.

A group of people would often come up to my job and speak with all hourly employees about joining their group to demand increased employee pay, respect, and fair treatment for all employees. I listened to their conversations but never joined as I didn't see a reason to do so (at the time). Not until what my manager said to me. I was taught throughout my life that no matter how much your emotions may fluctuate, ALWAYS try to do the right thing and uphold your morals as much as you possibly can. My manager called me into the office and scolded me for not leading and allowing my crewmate to stand beside me while on his phone. No matter how much I pleaded that it was intentional due to the circumstances of my crewmate, my manager wasn't listening. Then, my manager told me that I needed to learn how to "crack the whip" when work needed to be completed. This conversation and the rhetoric didn't sit well with me at all.

I pondered how the meeting went for a while and realized that the group of people trying to get us hourly employees to join their operation needed to be contacted. I spoke with them, and they began giving me the necessary information to push back against this type of dictatorship, as many hourly employees complained about unfair treatment. At this point, it just became louder as I started to see the world more broadly and stopped only worrying about myself and those I was responsible for. I became a monarch for those who didn't realize their power and had 60% of the employees join the fight. This was a massive issue for the company, and I faced a lot of adversity.

The location where I worked started to get more frequent visits from upper management, and many employees were laid off or fired for multiple reasons. Some of those employees joined me and the group I worked with in the fight for more income and equality. It's clear to say why they were targeted. From having another baby on the way, being a newlywed, watching those who stood by me be picked off, and receiving more work to do in hopes that I would fail, I had a lot of weight on me. Some days felt longer than others, and this place wasn't just my primary source of income but my only source of income. I was the primary source of income for my family as my wife couldn't work as much due to complications of the pregnancy. I was constantly being watched at my job due to my affiliations while trying to figure out my role as a husband. I realize I never had a good example of what a husband should be before I became a husband.

Trying to navigate being a husband and Father, being in constant fear of losing my employment, bickering with my Mother, siblings, and the Mothers of two of my children, and dealing with the death close to me was highly stressful at the time. All these fears and adversities were going on at once. At the same time, some positivity was also going on. My name was headlined in newspapers because I was speaking at different conferences around the U.S. My wife had my back (while also navigating through becoming a wife), and feeling the love and protection of GOD during these times kept me going. Despite all the mistakes and neglect, I realized that I showed those who mattered the most that I was driven by purpose and the desire to help.

We, the workers, eventually won the battle. As a result, increased wages and fair treatment working conditions were established nationwide. Knowing I was a major staple in helping with my struggles and what my coworkers were going through made me feel good. I climbed the corporate ladder, intending to put myself in a position of power to help and protect those who felt they didn't have a voice. Although my time with the company eventually ended, the experiences and gratitude from all the people I was able to connect with felt gratifying and fulfilling.

During my time there, it helped me to learn how to be a true leader. Most people think being a leader means being in charge and handling situations. Although it is a part of what makes a leader, it isn't the main ingredient. The most significant retrospective of being a leader is being a servant. To get all those different people from every walk of life to support me, I had to serve them. I was told that when you treat your employees/teammates well, they will walk through walls for you. I live by that model as I train and bring people on board. One of the greatest missions is helping and serving others when you can.

I touched on many situations I had to push through while working at my company and in my life. I realized more and more that I hadn't fully faced it yet. That situation is the death of those close to me. I've dealt with a few deaths that hurt me. Those deaths could make a person want to sit in depression and not continue for a while. In my case, it made me jump more into my work. I can admit that for some time, I never properly dealt with my grief and used work to "numb" me from my pain.

Death is one of the only things in life that we are guaranteed to experience. It is a naturally occurring event we often discover in our adolescence. Whether from seeing it on television or experiencing it in real life. Sometimes, we may have even died and brought back to life. I mean that both physically as well as mentally and emotionally. I've had my share of experiences on all levels.

My Father transitioned when I was three years old. There are many speculations as to what happened, but suicide is what is often mentioned. Growing up without a Father affected me in more ways than I realized. It wasn't until I was about thirty-one that I took in how I felt and everything that I lacked because of this. Throughout my years, I would randomly question how my life would be if he were around. It was the norm for me not to have him around. I genuinely believe it made me want to ensure I was in my children's lives. GOD placed multiple men in my life from whom I learned, and I am forever grateful. Three significant men are my Uncle, Donald Scott, my Apostle/Spiritual Father, Willie Cleveland, and my Mentor/Coach, Michael Bart Mathews. Being able to learn from them and having a listening ear about my issues as well as triumphs feels great.

Besides my Father's death, I've had my run-ins with death with people I never thought would be gone. I didn't start losing people close to me until my later years. I was in my mid-20s when death struck those that I was connected to, and I could feel the effect of losing bonds. With my Father, I can't recall our bond because of the time frame. I know he loved me, but I didn't have that bond. What did I do to cope with the many deaths that I experienced? I cried and worked through it.

From the year 2014 up until now, in 2024, I've lost many bonds. Friends, family, and even a mentee. Every death I've experienced hit me in different ways. Most were sudden, and I had no time to prepare. They just happened. My best friend's Father, my best friend, my Godmother, my sister, my paternal Great Aunt, one of my mentees, my maternal Aunt, and recently, my paternal Uncle all transitioned. Each person impacted my life while they were here and when they transitioned.

As I mentioned, most of them happened suddenly without preparation. Just pain and life afterward. My tears were shed, and my heartache was dealt with. I would talk to people about how it impacted me here and there, but I didn't dwell on it. I worked through it and tried to function daily as best as possible. My primary motivation was that my wife and children still needed me to provide for them. Dealing with each different death took different levels of mental and emotional strength especially depending on what was going on at the time. I had so much going on during these ten years.

Even with all that was transpiring, there is no permanent situation other than death. Reflecting on each person I mentioned confirms that you cherish those who matter to you. Their memory etched into the heart is how you keep them "alive." Continuing to be productive is how I honor their memory, as they wouldn't want me or anyone else to stop our lives on their behalf. I will take time to go through my memories with each of them, regardless of whether they brought smiles or tears. I suggest that everyone reading this passage also consider doing the same. Ask yourself, what would this person say to me if they could say something to me for thirty seconds? I guarantee the answer will be them telling you to push forward as they are rooting for you.

Time is a terrible thing to waste and something we can never get back, especially when a person isn't alive anymore. We can spend more time and learn from our errors, but we can never get those other moments back. The people (or persons) who value our time the most are our spouses (if applicable) and our children. I have a lot of children. Six, to be exact. Five biologically and one from my ended marriage. My biggest challenge was fighting for my right to be a Father. I've been in court battles since 2010 concerning my parenting, and an emotional rollercoaster still doesn't quite explain all the multitudes of highs and lows I experienced during those moments.

My oldest biological child was born in 2010. When her Mother and I ended the relationship, I thought that, at the time, court was the best route to take. I was young, dealing with the pain from an ended relationship, and becoming a Father for the first time had me in a whirlwind of doubt and uncertainty. The only thing I knew to do was not abandon my child. I had nieces and nephews, so the basics (diaper changing, bottle making, burping, etc.) were already in place.

The court battles started, and they were all ugly. I had the backing of my Mother, siblings, and friends, but it wasn't pleasant at all. Then, I had another daughter, and history repeated itself. Then, I discovered I had a son and wasn't aware he was mine. I discovered this after I thought it was my first biological son being born. I also had to go to court for my son, whom I wasn't aware of, to prove paternity. It was quick, and after discovering the truth, I immediately began being a Father to him as well. My family of six soon became seven, and then, after my last son was born, a family of eight. This occurred from 2010 to 2015.

Bickering, police involvement, ugly rhetoric, betrayal, and uncertainty were the primary wounds from the court battles. From 2010 to 2022, I was in court. Time and finances are the most significant losses from it all. There were some victories, like establishing joint custody and having a voice in the matters and affairs pertaining to my children. Three court battles concerning my children over twelve years were true madness. Although one ended quickly, the other two felt like they would never end.

Some days, I felt invincible; others, I felt like I didn't matter. I wasn't abusive, neglectful, or absent. I was present, and I provided. I know now that court should be a last resort if communication can't be established between both parents. I always ask people (especially fathers) who come to me for advice, or I randomly give advice. Have you tried communicating about everything before going this route? This question sparks a chain of self-reflection as communicating means both talking to give your perception and listening to understand.

I learned that doing the right thing and being present in your children's lives is what your children will remember. Showing up for birthdays and holidays, communicating throughout the week, and spending quality time is the key. Yes, having that legal protection is terrific, but reflecting on that time spent on "arguing" is dreadful. A good friend taught me that the wheels of justice are slow, but when they turn, the righteous are always in favor. In my case, it took twelve years for the "war" to be won, but it came with many casualties.

During most of my trials and tribulations of adulthood, I was married. We were married in 2015, and then we separated in 2023. The decision of divorce is still pending during the writing of this content. I had someone who was with me through it all. Although we're not together anymore, I do appreciate the companionship at that time. I learned many life lessons going through this process. I never thought I would see the day that this would happen. We went through it together: the good, the bad, the ugly, and the beautiful days.

Going through court battles, not following up after arguments, dealing with our families and their opinions, frequently traveling for jobs, and most importantly, not spending quality time with my wife and children are why we are where we are now. These are the things I reflected on as I aim to improve myself. It was a lot, and my actions and inactions contributed to us needing to walk away. I know it's not all my fault, but it's not my place to speak about what she did or didn't do because none of us are perfect, and we all have consistent growth to do.

Our current separation period is the worst experience of my life. Watching the person you would go to the moon and back for treat you as if you were the worst part of their life is devastating. Not to mention that many conversations couldn't be trusted. Uncertainty is in the picture until things are "settled." We may decide to reconcile and live life together again, but as of now, the divorce process is still ongoing. Getting to this decision-making point took a lot of reflection and prayer.

I was left with our children (her son and 'our' two sons) when she left our home. It was a mutual agreement for the children to stay with me for the remainder of the school year. I had to care for our children, run my business, work my job, battle adversity, heal my wounds, and rediscover myself all at the same time. That was a traumatic wake-up call for me! Most people call this period picking up the pieces of your life. I was shattered and all over the place. Am I fully put back together? No, I am not, but being driven by purpose and responsibility keeps me going.

My job and my business are the same. I mentor/coach people. It is truly my passion. Imagine doing that when you feel as though you have nothing to give and are in some of the worst pain in your life. I deal with about seventy people a week regarding coaching and mentoring. The age range varies as the youngest mentee I serviced was five, and the oldest was fifty-five. This was a true challenge as I was the person that most people came to for help. Borrowing money, advice, a car ride, and most importantly, just being there for people in general, which usually meant them venting.

Dealing with seventy people a week is no small task. I work with five appointed advocates to service the youth I encounter, and it's a huge help. Ultimately, I still oversee them all. Not to mention that I have my (own) mentees as well. Sixteen, to be exact, at this time. Having to find the strength to pour into others weekly while feeling anxiety, dealing with intrusive thoughts, and just overall sad was the worst. Not to mention dealing with the trauma from the adversities I was facing at the time.

One night, my car was broken into while I was gathering my things from a friend's house to move back into my home (I left briefly at the initial separation) to get my children. The perpetrators ram shacked my car and took some crucial items from me. They stole my book bag, which contained all my work and laptop. I was devastated as I had a lot of essential files in my bookbag. I never expected to be robbed. This caused a significant strain on me as I had to report to the authorities and my job of the incident. I also had to prepare myself mentally to recover all the stolen information. Several days went by, and I heard GOD tell me to go back and search the area where my car was vandalized. I listened and located everything thrown under a dumpster. My laptop wasn't recovered, but I had a win as I was able to reclaim the work I had missed.

My children were getting into situations left and right, especially my oldest son. Their schools were contacting me back to back about behavioral issues and inappropriate social media. Of course, their mothers and I cooperated to get them back in order, but the timing was impeccable. I was, again, dealing with everything while at one of the lowest points in my life, and it felt like a streak of bad luck. I held to my beliefs/faith and was able to conquer this situation as well. My children are getting better daily, and I am proud of them.

Then, I was bombarded with people upset with me about not wanting to work with them any longer. False accusations and defamation of my character were strong. I had to have meetings and was investigated to ensure those accusations were untrue. I gained people who were set out to destroy me, but all I wanted to do was ensure we were always doing the right thing. Is the situation over? I can't necessarily say, but I refuse to envelop myself in the madness. Praying for truth, keeping my composure, and not having any animosity towards them kept me at peace internally. Not to mention that my marriage status was heavy on my mind and heart, so it negated that panic mostly.

Dealing with a heavy heart and back-to-back situations occurring had me stressing out. Stress also shows up on the outside and can affect you in so many ways. I was drained and tired a lot, but I couldn't sleep. One day, that lack of rest caught up and overtook my mind. While I was driving, I passed out. Thank GOD I was going less than ten miles per hour, so I wasn't harmed when I ran into the pole. My car was damaged, but I had my life, and no one was harmed. The hood and latch were destroyed as well. I had no clue that the hood latch wasn't holding, and when I went over twenty miles per hour, it flew up and shattered my window. The worst luck ever was still happening, but again, I looked toward the positive.

Heartbreak is horrible, and the pain is only curable over time. Even when you heal, it still leaves behind scarred tissue. The healing happens when you focus on yourself and that which you can control. I discovered this and began that process amid everything happening. From my car broken into to my damaged vehicle, I was doing what was necessary to focus on myself along the Pathway To Trauma Recovery.

How someone heals looks different for everyone, but it's worth it if you do it correctly. Focusing on myself (self-care) began my healing process. I did that by getting in tune with GOD, exercising and changing my diet, being more present for my children, reading more, setting boundaries, and fulfilling my purpose by helping others through mentoring. The chaos and turmoil I went through for what seemed like forever conditioned me to be the best version of myself. As time passes, I will continue to improve at what is important to me. I hope everyone remembers this as you continue your self-care techniques.

Run towards your FAITH/BELIEFS, and everyone and everything meant for you will be attractive to you. Get to know and call upon your Higher Power during good times and not-so-good times. There is a power source that spans every corner of the Universe to infinity and beyond. Tune in, Tapp in, and get Turned on to that spiritual power source.

Some call it High Power, God, Allah, Jehovah, Elohim, Most High, Father, Alfa and Omega, and more. Your spiritual journey (or not) is your choice.

ABOUT THE AUTHOR

RAYSHUN SCOTT

My name is Rayshaun Scott (but you can call me Ray), and I am thirty-three years old. I have six beautiful children (Lavacea, Rashiya, Riley, Uziya, Rayshaun Jr., and Ryan), whom I love and adore with every fiber of my being. We live in the State of Illinois.

I am the youngest on both sides of my family, with nine siblings. I was born and raised on the mighty Southside of Chicago. Starting with my education from the mean streets, I learned about surviving and not getting caught up. Then, I moved on to my parental lessons, the Chicago Public School education, and the many spiritual leaders I have encountered. I attended both Tarkington and Hurley Elementary schools from Pre-K through 8th grade. I received my diploma from Bogan High School and studied in a higher learning education course at IADT International Academy of Design & Technology and Westwood College.

Throughout my entire experience (home, streets of Chicago, High School, college, jobs, and my spiritual path), I learned to be open to all cultures and religious practices. All religions are important, and no one religion is greater than the other.

Since I was younger, I have always had a connection with GOD. I was taught how to pray by my Mother and my older siblings. My Aunt Dolores would take me to church with her whenever I visited. I refer to and use (the name) GOD because I am comfortable calling HIM/HER/IT, etc. My wife was the person who fully got me into the church when she introduced me to Mount Zion Temple of Deliverance, which she attended at the time. I am a member of the church, but I am not religious. I am more into spirituality, which is why I say no religion is better than the other. My church certainly helps with the feeding and nourishment of my soul.

I worked for a company for nearly ten years (2012 through 2021). During that time, I was "activated" and began my journey into seeing life with fewer filters and becoming more of a leader. At this job, I participated in multiple protests and spoke at a few seminars (once at church and even in Washington, D.C.) during my career. After hearing the different crowds' reactions and my mentors telling me how well-spoken I was, I knew that public speaking was my passion.

After working my way up through the company's corporate ladder and becoming a salaried management team member, I began stepping more into my destiny of ministering and coaching. I made it my goal to pull up as many people as possible. Whether financially, spiritually, physically, emotionally, or mentally, I wanted to help those in need and those who wanted my help. Today, I am an entrepreneur with my business up and running, which involves mentoring and coaching people of all ages and working at a company focused on youth advocacy. My accreditations and certifications allow me to coach/mentor all ages nationally. I also work with other companies and organizations with like-minded missions like mine.

Contact me: https://dot.cards/weaspeople.

The Mathews Entrepreneur Group Inc
We Create Books Division
www.tmeginc.com

Michael Bart Mathews
Email: wecreatebooks@tmeginc
Direct: 1/708/634/6785

www.ingramcontent.com/pod-product-compliance
Lightning Source LLC
Chambersburg PA
CBHW051523150726
47997CB00001B/365